Longman Study Texts

Poetry

Longman Study Texts

General editor: Richard Adams

Titles in the series:

Jane Austen
Emma
Pride and Prejudice
Charlotte Bronte
Jane Eyre
Emily Bronte
Wuthering Heights
Charles Dickens
Great Expectations
Oliver Twist
George Eliot
Silas Marner
The Mill on the Floss
Thomas Hardy
The Mayor of Casterbridge
Aldous Huxley
Brave New World
D H Lawrence
Sons and Lovers
George Orwell
Animal Farm
Nineteen Eighty-Four
Paul Scott
Staying On
Virginia Woolf
To the Lighthouse
Oliver Goldsmith
She Stoops to Conquer
Nadine Gordimer
July's People
Ben Jonson
Volpone
Christopher Marlowe
Doctor Faustus
Somerset Maugham
Short Stories

Alan Paton
Cry, the Beloved Country
Terence Rattigan
The Winslow Boy
Willy Russell
Educating Rita
Peter Shaffer
Amadeus
Equus
The Royal Hunt of the Sun
William Shakespeare
Macbeth
The Merchant of Venice
Romeo and Juliet
Richard Brinsley Sheridan
The Rivals
The School for Scandal
John Webster
The White Devil
The Duchess of Malfi

Bernard Shaw
Androcles and the Lion
Arms and the Man
Caesar and Cleopatra
The Devil's Disciple
Major Barbara
Pygmalion
St Joan
H G Wells
The History of Mr Polly
Oscar Wilde
The Importance of Being Earnest
Robin Jenkins
The Cone-Gatherers
J B Priestley
An Inspector Calls

Editor: George MacBeth
Poetry for Today
Editor: Michael Marland
Short Stories for Today

Editor: George MacBeth

Poetry for Today

Longman

LONGMAN GROUP UK LIMITED
Longman House
Burnt Mill, Harlow, Essex, CM20 2JE, England
and Associated Companies throughout the world

© Longman Group Limited 1984

First published 1984
Second impression 1987
ISBN 0 582 33144 7

Set in 10/12 Linotron Baskerville

Produced by Longman Group (FE) Ltd
Printed in Hong Kong

Contents

page

Foreword

There are ten poets in this anthology, three of them dead, and, of the remaining seven, one is over seventy and four are under forty. Two of the best, the poet laureate (which means crowned with laurel) Sir John Betjeman and the Yorkshire poet Ted Hughes, write verse which is bound to appeal to those who enjoy and admire the English countryside, in all its violence, and with all its nostalgic power to remind us of the past.

Of the others, however, D H Lawrence was the son of a Nottingham miner, Stevie Smith worked as a London secretary, and Ai is the daughter of black American and Japanese parents in Arizona. None of them concentrate on the English country-side. Nor, indeed, do the remaining five poets.

Kit Wright is a poet and songwriter whose *Elizabeth* is a subtle comment on race prejudice in the United States. Brian Patten is a Liverpool-born poet who can pluck the strings of passion *Somewhere between Heaven and Woolworth's*. Paul Muldoon lives and works at the heart of our most acute political crisis, in Ulster, and his poem *Immram* uses the techniques of the TV gangster movie to say something about the relationship between fathers and sons.

Philip Larkin is a librarian in Hull. In a poem like *Homage to a Government* he can touch on the bitterness a lot of people feel about our country's changed role in the world. And Vachel Lindsay, in his elemental poem *The Congo*, which raps along to the beat of an invisible tom-tom, has a lot to say about the myth-springs of black (and other) nationalisms.

These are the poets, men and women, black and white. All from different backgrounds, and all writing in English as their mother tongue. What they make of it is what *you* can make of it. The ways they find to express what they think and feel about our modern world are ways available to anyone. There is nothing elitist or exclusive about them.

Philip Larkin and Vachel Lindsay write with the rhyming wit

and rhythm of Pam Ayres or John Cooper Clarke. D H Lawrence and Ai write with the free directness of Bob Dylan or Mick Jagger.

The only difference between a good poet and a good singer is that a good poet never needs a backing group. His or her voice carries its own built-in music. This book will try to show you how, and to teach you how to do the same thing – in however small a way – for yourself.

How to write a poem

The most important thing to say about writing a poem is that it doesn't need to be a poem. Write what you want to write, and then make it a poem later. It may even be a poem already. Much of the time, what separates a poem from a piece of prose is merely the point at which the lines stop before they reach the edge of the page. That, and the spaces between groups of lines.

A piece of prose normally has ideas arranged in sentences with punctuation – full stops, commas and so on – put in to make the meaning clearer. The sentences are usually grouped in paragraphs, each indicated by starting its opening word a few spaces in from the left-hand edge of the page. The distance between the last word in each line and the edge of the page is a matter decided by the printer, not the author, and it has no relevance to the meaning, or the rhythm, of the sentence in which it appears. Indeed, the last word is occasionally broken in the middle, and marked with a hyphen.

The easiest way to turn a piece of prose into a poem is simply to take something already written and arrange the ends of the lines and the spaces between the lines in a new way. It can be any way you like. Whatever way it is, you will be surprised how easy it is to accept the resulting piece as 'a poem', something that seems to have a flavour of its own, and demands to be spoken aloud and thought about.

For a start, you might like to choose any passage from this introduction. Later on, you can try something from a newspaper, or the *TV Times*, or a few sentences from a letter, or a caption from *Woman's Own*, or an extract from a story in *Mayfair*. Later, you can write something yourself, as a piece of prose, and then re-arrange that.

Let me show you what I mean with a few of my own lines. Here is a re-arrangement of the first few sentences of this section:

The most important thing to
say about writing a poem
is that it doesn't need
to be a poem. Write

what you want to write,
and then make it a
poem later. It may even
be a poem already.

I could go on indefinitely. Try for yourself. You'll soon find that
it sounds better the more you break up the phrases and avoid
the natural conversational groups; and you'll also find that
there's more than one way you can arrange any particular set of
words. Here is a variant on my first few sentences:

The most important
thing to
say about
writing a
poem
is that it
doesn't

need to be
a poem. Write
what you
want to
write, and
then make
it

... and so on. Here's another variant, this time not having all
the lines about the same length but making alternate ones the
same.

The most important thing to say about writing a poem
   is that it
doesn't need to be a poem. Write what you want to
   write, and then
make it a poem later. It may even be a poem

already. Much of the time, what separates a poem from
   a piece

... and so on. Why don't you take the third paragraph of this section and see what you can do with that? After you've re-arranged some lines, try varying the punctuation, and see what fun you can have with that. Here is an example, again from my first paragraph:

'The most important thing to
say about (writing?) a poem
is that it *doesn't* need
to be a poem.' WRITE

WHAT YOU WANT TO. Write,
and then 'make' it a
poem, later. It may even
be a poem – already!

I've overdone the punctuation here, but it does show how the feeling of the piece can be made to vary. It can get more excitable, more unsure of itself, more thoughtful, more indirect.

As a reverse exercise, try putting one of the poems in this book back (back?) into prose. Here are a few lines of Paul Muldoon's *Immram*, to show you what I mean:

I was fairly and squarely behind the eight that morning in Foster's pool-hall when it came to me out of the blue in the shape of a sixteen-ounce billiard cue that lent what he said some little weight. 'Your old man was an ass-hole. That makes an ass-hole out of you.' My grand-father hailed from New York State. My grand-mother was part Cree. This must be some new strain in my pedigree.

As soon as you've done this, you can see why he put the poem in the other arrangement to begin with. It makes the rhymes clearer, for instance. But your new prose arrangement may help, for a moment, to bring out the gangster story style which lies behind the poem's method. We're more used to that in prose – in a magazine or when spoken in a TV serial.

You might like to try imitating the Muldoon poem. Make up a crime story – perhaps about a gang making a stick-up raid on a bank – and then arrange what you've written in groups of ten lines, as Paul Muldoon does in *Immram*. Try making the last two words in the last two lines rhyme, or at least have something in common. They might just both have an 's' at the end, or the same vowel. Then give your poem a title, the name of one of your robbers perhaps. Make it a very unusual name: not Bill or David or Smith or Jones. Call him Chevrolet or Kittycat or Wilberforce; anything, so long as it seems unusual.

After this, you might like to try inventing a longer series of unusual names. How about making up names for the top ten bands in 1990? Think about Depeche Mode, The Police, Altered Images, Whitesnake. Can you do better? Make your list as absurd and unusual as you can. Then take any one of your names and try to find as many rhymes as you can for the last word in it.

Suppose you have a band called Peanut Butter: there's flutter, shutter, shut her, cut her, mutter, nutter; then there are things that sound nearly the same, or perhaps exactly the same in some accents, like put her, shoot here, suitor, cuter, scooter; and words that don't exactly rhyme but sound similar, like floater, bitter, batter, boater, bloater, beater, biter. When you start looking out for those you'll soon see that almost any word can have lots of others to 'rhyme' with it. This makes writing poems that rhyme very easy.

You might like to try doing an imitation of one of John Betjeman's poems; *Trebetherick*, for instance. Why not take all his rhyme words, in the same order (thrift, edge, drift, ledge) and then slightly change them so that you get, for example, throat, sludge, draught, itch. Then try writing your own seaside poem using your new words as rhymes, and keeping his line-groupings (forget about the metre). Here's the sort of thing I mean:

I always used to get an awfully sore throat
    When I got my feet wet in the sludge.
It was just the same whenever I stood in a draught
    And it was always followed up by an itch.
Worst of all, my parents always laughed
    Whenever my trousers needed a hitch
From standing barefooted with my big toe
In seaweed. My father looked up and said: what
Are doing, boy? Give me some more tea. So
I poured him a cup and thought I ought to sugar it.

Not very good, is it? You could do better than that. The thing is not to mind if you find you end up writing nonsense. Nonsense that rhymes is often very good fun. You can learn how to write sense that rhymes later, when you've had more practice.

Why not get some practice by trying to put one of Ai's poems into rhyme? Or take one of Stevie Smith's poems out of rhyme? Here is an example:

High up
In the attic
Sits Croft.
He has a screw loose.

These changes – turning things upside down, moving bits and pieces about – will soon begin to show you, perhaps better than reading and thinking, how a particular poem works, and why the poet wrote it just as it is.

Understanding a poem isn't, after all, so very different from knowing how to knit, or how to drive a car. When you can cast off, or change a tyre, you're more able to appreciate a Fair Isle sweater or know what makes a Lotus corner well. You can use your eyes, and enjoy well-knitted woollen goods, or well-designed motor cars, but you'll know more about them, if you can mend a tear, or drain a radiator. There may be some jobs only the skilled seamstress or the trained mechanic can do; but quite a few are within the reach of the ordinary person. The same goes for poems. Not all of us could write *The Congo*, or *The Bull Moses*; but we can all learn to line and rhyme something, and thus learn the process which leads to the greatness.

Finally, tunes: all poems have a rhythm to them. It may be the kind of prosy one I've been stressing so far, or it may be a much more regular, song-like one, such as Kit Wright uses in *Elizabeth*. Very often in English you can get a good lilting rhythm and make your poem sound natural, by using what the books call 'dactyls'.

These aren't a new kind of dinosaur, and there's no need to be frightened of them. Here's a batch I've made up:

Christmas is   coming and   what shall I   do?
Shall I give   presents to   all of my   friends?
Yes, I shall   give them all   lots of nice   things.
Treacle and   chestnuts and   pork pie and   jam.

Not difficult to pick up, is it? One two three, one two three, one two three four; one two three, one two three, one two three four. You might find it easier to do if you get up and dance while you say the words aloud. Exactly. You've got it! It's a kind of waltz rhythm.

You might like to try writing a poem about Easter using this rhythm. Write out the words in groups to isolate each phrase of the rhythm and you'll find it easy. Here is an example:

Easter is when Jesus Christ was once killed.

Again, it's not very good. You could do better. If you're feeling really clever you might like to combine this rhythm – these dactyls – with some rhymes at the end of lines. Once you've done this you'll be a pretty sophisticated poet, and you won't need to learn a lot more from me. It will become simply a matter of practice – getting better and better.

Working at not wasting words. Learning to compare one thing with another. Trying to sound like yourself and not like someone else.

These last three things are all more difficult, and must come with time. But the most important of all – at least the great Greek critic Aristotle (rhymes with bottle) thought so – is making comparisons; seeing how one thing is like another, and in a new way.

Take a look at Lawrence's *Mosquito*, to see how well this kind of thing can be done. But don't despair. There are all sorts of short-cuts to help you get that kind of surprise effect for yourself. Comparison games will often train your wits for this. For example: make two lists of nouns, and keep them separate. They might be: book, lion, nutshell; telephone, fire, butter. Now take the first noun in the first list and the first noun in the second list and form a question with them, like this:

Why is a good book like a telephone? Why is a good lion like a fire? Why is a good nutshell like butter?

Now think of an answer to each question. It doesn't matter how silly it is, as long as it emphasizes one thing the two have in common. For example: A good book is like a telephone because both are hard, or silent, or something you can hold, or likely to spoil when they get wet.

Now you can use your comparison in a short poem. For example:

The good book, like a telephone, resists my hand.
It says nothing.
I can lift it up.
Like a telephone,
The good book is ruined by rain.

Try doing the same with why a good lion is like a fire. Very soon you'll become quite expert at twisting things round. Use all my earlier tips, too. When you've got your four sentences written, try re-arranging them in lines – or try arranging them in waltz time.

The good book, like a
telephone, resists
my hand. It says

nothing. I can lift
it up. Like a
telephone

the good book
is ruined
by rain.

Or:

Telephone!   Yes, the good   book is like   that.
Nothing it   says but it   presses my   hand.

Of course, these are trivial sorts of comparison. The great blaze of metaphor usually works in much grander terms. But the arbitrary – the quirky, unique, strained quality – is often nearer to the heart of it. You can more easily hit on a good comparison by going too far than by not going far enough.

Why not read this introduction through again, and try out some of the ideas it suggests? Don't just follow through parrot fashion, though. Develop ideas of your own. Remember always, when you write your own work, those two rules I mentioned but didn't illustrate: Don't waste words. Be yourself.

Vachel Lindsay

The American poet Vachel Lindsay was born in 1879 in Springfield, Illinois. Earlier in the century the great American president, Abraham Lincoln, who fought the Civil War on the issue of black slavery, had also been born in Springfield, and the association with Lincoln was very important for Lindsay. The poet's father was a doctor, and Vachel was educated at Hiram College, and at the Chicago and New York art schools. He designed illustrations for his own poems and wrote one of the earliest books on the cinema, *The Art of the Moving Picture*, in 1916. In the same year, he wrote another prose book, based on his experiences as a wandering minstrel who often had to sing for his supper: *A Handy Guide for Beggars*.

Vachel Lindsay was the first poet to make a consistent living as a reader of his own verse to large public audiences, and, as such, he is the predecessor of thousands of living poets and poet-singers from Bob Dylan to Allen Ginsberg. Lindsay was a deeply religious man, with a profound interest in mass rituals (those of ancient Egypt as well as those on the cinema screen). His best poems, like *The Congo*, were vehicles for a common involvement in serious themes. With all the forcefulness of an orator, like the black social rights leader Martin Luther King or the Cuban president Fidel Castro, Lindsay could whip up large audiences into a fervour of enthusiasm. He did this neither with the plain prose of the politician, nor the guitar-backed vocalization of the blues singer. He did it entirely with the basic rhetoric of rhyme. His power lay in his poetry.

VACHEL LINDSAY

The Congo

A STUDY OF THE NEGRO RACE

(Being a memorial to Ray Eldred, a Disciple missionary of
the Congo River)

I. THEIR BASIC SAVAGERY

Fat black bucks in a wine-barrel
    room,
Barrel-house kings, with feet
    unstable,
Sagged and reeled and pounded   *A deep rolling bass.*
    on the table,
Pounded on the table,
Beat an empty barrel with the
    handle of a broom,
Hard as they were able,
Boom, boom, BOOM,
With a silk umbrella and the
    handle of a broom,
Boomlay, boomlay, boomlay,
    BOOM.
THEN I had religion, THEN I
    had a vision.
I could not turn from their revel
    in derision.
THEN I SAW THE CONGO,   *More deliberate.*
    CREEPING   *Solemnly chanted.*
    THROUGH THE
    BLACK,
CUTTING THROUGH THE
    FOREST WITH A
    GOLDEN TRACK.

VACHEL LINDSAY

Then along that riverbank
A thousand miles
Tattooed cannibals danced in
    files;
Then I heard the boom of the
    blood-lust song
And a thigh-bone beating on a   *A rapidly piling climax*
    tin-pan gong.   *of speed and racket.*
And 'BLOOD' screamed the
    whistles and the fifes of
    the warriors,
'BLOOD' screamed the
    skull-faced, lean
    witch-doctors,
'Whirl ye the deadly voo-doo
    rattle,
Harry the uplands,
Steal all the cattle,
Rattle-rattle, rattle-rattle,
Bing.
Boomlay, boomlay, boomlay,
    BOOM,'
A roaring, epic, rag-time tune   *With a philosophic*
From the mouth of the Congo   *pause.*
To the Mountains of the Moon.
Death is an Elephant,
Torch-eyed and horrible,   *Shrilly and with a*
Foam-flanked and terrible.   *heavily accented metre.*
BOOM, steal the pygmies,
BOOM, kill the Arabs,
BOOM, kill the white men,
HOO, HOO, HOO.
Listen to the yell of Leopold's   *Like the wind in the*
    ghost   *chimney.*

3

Burning in Hell for his
    hand-maimed host.
Hear how the demons chuckle
    and yell
Cutting his hands off, down in
    Hell.
Listen to the creepy
    proclamation,
Blown through the lairs of the
    forest-nation,
Blown past the white-ants' hill
    of clay,
Blown past the marsh where the
    butterflies play: –
'Be careful what you do,
Or Mumbo-Jumbo, God of   *All the 'o' sounds very*
    the Congo,   *golden. Heavy accents*
And all of the other   *very heavy. Light*
Gods of the Congo,   *accents very light. Last*
Mumbo-Jumbo will hoo-doo   *line whispered.*
    you,
Mumbo-Jumbo will hoo-doo
    you,
Mumbo-Jumbo will hoo-doo
    you.'

II. THEIR IRREPRESSIBLE HIGH SPIRITS

Wild crap-shooters with a   *Rather shrill and high.*
    whoop and a call
Danced the juba in their
    gambling hall
And laughed fit to kill, and
    shook the town,

And guyed the policemen and
    laughed them down
With a boomlay, boomlay,
    boomlay, BOOM.
THEN I SAW THE CONGO,   *Read exactly as in first*
    CREEPING   *section.*
    THROUGH THE
    BLACK,
CUTTING THROUGH THE
    FOREST WITH A
    GOLDEN TRACK.

A negro fairyland swung into   *Lay emphasis on the*
    view,   *delicate ideas. Keep as*
A minstrel river   *light-footed as possible.*
Where dreams come true.
The ebony palace soared on
    high
Through the blossoming trees to
    the evening sky.
The inlaid porches and
    casements shone
With gold and ivory and
    elephant-bone.
And the black crowd laughed till
    their sides were sore
At the baboon butler in the
    agate door,
And the well-known tunes of the
    parrot band
That trilled on the bushes of
    that magic land.

A troupe of skull-faced   *With pomposity.*
    witch-men came

Through the agate doorway in
    suits of flame,
Yea, long-tailed coats with a
    gold-leaf crust
And hats that were covered with
    diamond-dust.
And the crowd in the court gave
    a whoop and a call
And danced the juba from wall
    to wall.

But the witch-men suddenly   *With a great*
    stilled the throng   *deliberation and*
With a stern cold glare, and a   *ghostliness.*
    stern old song: –
'Mumbo-Jumbo will hoo-doo
    you.'. . .

Just then from the doorway, as   *With over-whelming*
    fat as shotes,   *assurance, good cheer,*
Came the cake-walk princes in   *and pomp.*
    their long red coats,
Canes with a brilliant lacquer
    shine,
And tall silk hats that were red
    as wine.

And they pranced with their   *With growing speed*
    butterfly partners there,   *and sharply marked*
Coal-black maidens with pearls   *dance-rhythm.*
    in their hair,
Knee-skirts trimmed with the
    jessamine sweet,
And bells on their ankles and
    little black-feet.

And the couples railed at the
    chant and the frown
Of the witch-men lean, and
    laughed them down.
(Oh, rare was the revel, and well
    worth while
That made those glowering
    witch-men smile.)

The cake-walk royalty then
    began
To walk for a cake that was tall
    as a man
To the tune of 'Boomlay,
    boomlay, BOOM,'
While the witch-men laughed,
    with a sinister air,   *With a touch of negro*
And sang with the scalawags   *dialect, and as rapidly*
    prancing there: –   *as possible toward the*
    end.
'Walk with care, walk with care,
Or Mumbo-Jumbo, God of the
    Congo,
And all of the other Gods of the
    Congo,
Mumbo-Jumbo will hoo-doo
    you.
Beware, beware, walk with care,
Boomlay, boomlay, boomlay,
    boom.
Boomlay, boomlay, boomlay,
    boom.
Boomlay, boomlay, boomlay,
    boom.

7

Boomlay, boomlay, boomlay,
  BOOM.'
(Oh, rare was the revel, and well   *Slow philosophic calm.*
    worth while
That made those glowering
    witch-men smile.)

III. THE HOPE OF THEIR RELIGION

A good old negro in the slums of   *Heavy bass. With a*
    the town   *literal imitation of*
Preached at a sister for her   *camp-meeting racket,*
    velvet gown.   *and trance.*
Howled at a brother for his
    low-down ways,
His prowling, guzzling,
    sneak-thief days.
Beat on the Bible till he wore it
    out
Starting the jubilee revival
    shout.
And some had visions, as they
    stood on chairs,
And sang of Jacob, and the
    golden stairs,
And they all repented, a
    thousand strong
From their stupor and savagery
    and sin and wrong
And slammed with their hymn
    books till they shook the
    room
With 'glory, glory, glory,'
And 'Boom, boom, BOOM.'

THEN I SAW THE CONGO,
     CREEPING
     THROUGH THE
     BLACK,
CUTTING THROUGH THE
     JUNGLE WITH A
     GOLDEN TRACK.

*Exactly as in the first
section. Begin with
terror and power, end
with joy.*

And the gray sky opened like a
     new-rent veil
And showed the Apostles with
     their coats of mail.
In bright white steel they were
     seated round
And their fire-eyes watched
     where the Congo wound.
And the twelve Apostles, from
     their thrones on high
Thrilled all the forest with their
     heavenly cry: –
'Mumbo-Jumbo will die in the
     jungle;
Never again will he hoo-doo
     you,
Never again will he hoo-doo
     you.'

*Sung to the tune of
'Hark, ten thousand
harps and voices'.*

Then along that river, a
     thousand miles
The vine-snared trees fell down
     in files.
Pioneer angels cleared the way
For a Congo paradise, for babes
     at play,

*With growing
deliberation and joy.*

9

For sacred capitals, for temples
    clean.
Gone were the skull-faced
    witch-men lean.
There, where the wild   *In a rather high key –*
    ghost-gods had wailed   *as delicately as possible.*
A million boats of the angels
    sailed
With oars of silver, and prows of
    blue
And silken pennants that the
    sun shone through.
'Twas a land transfigured, 'twas
    a new creation.
Oh, a singing wind swept the
    negro nation
And on through the backwoods
    clearing flew: –
'Mumbo-Jumbo is dead in the   *To the tune of 'Hark,*
    jungle.   *ten thousand harps and*
Never again will he hoo-doo   *voices'.*
    you.
Never again will he hoo-doo
    you.'

Redeemed were the forests, the
    beasts and the men,
And only the vulture dared
    again
By the far, lone mountains of the
    moon
To cry, in the silence, the Congo
    tune: –

Mumbo-Jumbo will hoo-doo you,
   'Mumbo-Jumbo will hoo-doo
      you.
   Mumbo ... Jumbo ... will ...
      hoo-doo ... you.'

Dying down into a penetrating, terrified whisper.

This poem, particularly the third section, was suggested by an allusion in a sermon by my pastor, F W Burnham, to the heroic life and death of Ray Eldred. Eldred was a missionary of the Disciples of Christ who perished while swimming a treacherous branch of the Congo. See *A Master Builder on the Congo*, by Andrew F Henesey, published by Fleming H Revell.

Daniel

(Inscribed to Isador Bennett Reed)

Darius the Mede was a king and
    a wonder.   *Beginning with a strain*
                                       of 'Dixie'.
His eye was proud, and his voice
    was thunder.
He kept bad lions in a monstrous
    den.
He fed up the lions on Christian
    men.
Daniel was the chief hired man of   *With a touch of*
    the land.   *'Alexander's Band'.*
He stirred up the jazz in the palace
    band.
He whitewashed the cellar. He
    shovelled in the coal.
And Daniel kept a-praying: – 'Lord save my soul.'
Daniel kept a-praying 'Lord save my soul.'
Daniel kept a-praying 'Lord save my soul.'

Daniel was the butler, swagger and swell.
He ran up stairs. He answered the bell.
And *he* would let in whoever came a-calling: –
Saints so holy, scamps so appalling.
'Old man Ahab leaves his card.
Elisha and the bears are a-waiting in the yard.
Here comes Pharaoh and his snakes a-calling.
Here comes Cain and his wife a-calling.
Shadrach, Meshach and Abednego for tea.
Here comes Jonah and the whale,
And the *Sea!*
Here comes St Peter and his fishing pole.

Here comes Judas and his silver a-calling.
Here comes old Beelzebub a-calling.'
And Daniel kept a-praying: – 'Lord save my soul.'
Daniel kept a-praying: – 'Lord save my soul.'
Daniel kept a-praying: – 'Lord save my soul.'

His sweetheart and his mother were Christian and
      meek.
They washed and ironed for Darius every week.
One Thursday he met them at the door: –
Paid them as usual, but acted sore.

He said: – 'Your Daniel is a dead little pigeon.
He's a good hard worker, but he talks religion.'
And he showed them Daniel in the lions' cage.
Daniel standing quietly, the lions in a rage.
His good old mother cried: –
'Lord save him.'
And Daniel's tender sweetheart cried: –
'Lord save him.'
And she was a golden lily in the dew.
And she was as sweet as an apple on the tree
And she was as fine as a melon in the corn-field,
Gliding and lovely as a ship on the sea,
Gliding and lovely as a ship on the sea.

And she prayed to the Lord: –
'Send Gabriel. Send Gabriel.'

King Darius said to the lions: –
'Bite Daniel. Bite Daniel.
Bite him. Bite him. Bite him!'

Thus roared the lions: –
'We want Daniel, Daniel, Daniel,
We want Daniel, Daniel, Daniel.
G rrrrrrrrrrrrrrrrrrrrrrrrrrrrrrrrrrrrrrrr *Here the audience roars*
G rrrrrrrrrrrrrrrrrrrrrrrrrrrrrrrrrrrrrrr.' *with the leader.*

And Daniel did not frown,
Daniel did not cry.
He kept on looking at the sky.
And the Lord said to Gabriel: –
'Go chain the lions down,   *The audience sings this*
Go chain the lions down.   *with the leader, to the old*
Go chain the lions down.   *negro tune.*
Go chain the lions down.'

And *Gabriel* chained the lions,
And *Gabriel* chained the lions,
And *Gabriel* chained the lions,
And Daniel got out of the den,
And Daniel got out of the den,
And Daniel got out of the den.
And Darius said: – 'You're a
      Christian child,'
Darius said: – 'You're a Christian
      child,'
Darius said: – 'You're a Christian
      child,'
And gave him his job again,
And gave him his job again,
And gave him his job again.

Factory Windows Are Always Broken

Factory windows are always broken.
Somebody's always throwing bricks,
Somebody's always heaving cinders,
Playing ugly Yahoo tricks.

Factory windows are always broken.
Other windows are let alone.
No one throws through the chapel-window
The bitter, snarling, derisive stone.

Factory windows are always broken.
Something or other is going wrong.
Something is rotten – I think, in Denmark.
End of the factory-window song.

Notes

The Congo

The Congo is the longest poem in this book. It carries the subtitle 'a study of the negro race', and this in itself, coming as the poem does from a white man, may be enough to damn it unread. Those who pass on to the first few lines may be quickly shocked by the title of section one THEIR BASIC SAVAGERY and the opening words 'fat black bucks'. But read on. The headlong flood of the rhythm will pretty quickly get a grip on you. Feel the surge and bang of the words as you read them aloud. Aloud, because this is not a poem which will yield up much interest if quietly mouthed over in a hushed monotone, or murmured only for the inner ear. It needs to be YELLED. Or rather it needs to be spoken with all the variations of tone and speed that Vachel Lindsay himself so helpfully sets out in the margin. This isn't just a poem. It's a musical score. So settle back and try it out. You may first hear the poem read by your teacher, who will attempt to convey as much of the force and range of the rhythm as he or she can. But the next thing is to try some of the poem for yourself. Let the words come alive in your own mouth. Doesn't it feel good to have all that energy and amazement bubbling up out of your own throat? Can't you feel the sweep and bump of the verse in your own guts? No? Well, turn to Ai, and come back later. But if you *can* feel it, yield to it. Go with the poem. Let it ride you for a while. This isn't a poem to be stopped and pawed over for every little local pleasure or groped through for every minor occasional flaw. It's a big, rushing poem. A poem to be taken and swallowed. By the end you may feel exhausted, or disgusted; but you'll hardly be unmoved. Once you've got right through, stop and take stock. Think for yourself. Is this a bigoted, anti-black poem? Is it the kind of poem that does harm to race relations? Or does it have the honesty to say what it feels, and (even more) to express what it thinks? Need it, after all, even be about black people at all? Isn't there a sort of elemental interest here in primitive tribal force and the extent to which that must be curbed by law and principle, whether that force is black or white or any other colour? Remember, too, that it was Vachel Lindsay, in the mid 1920s, who started the black American poet Langston Hughes on his career when he met him working as a bag-boy in a hotel. Yes, but is that relevant? Might that not have been the typical helpful gesture of a guilty liberal? Read the poem through again, preferably sharing out parts through the class, and then have a general discussion about the issues which it raises.

Daniel

This is a poem to be spoken in public, with groups of lines shared out. The effect, as you'll find, is very invigorating and lively. On the page, it's a rumbustious, comic piece, which may not seem to mean much. Spoken with a group of other people, it takes on the force of a college football chant, or a church service including hymns and prayers. In America – at Vachel Lindsay's own school, Hiram College, for example – there are many traditional college chants which are designed to be spoken, often whispered, in public by a huge crowd, and whose effect is akin to that of national anthems, lauding the virtues, albeit often with humour, of a particular community or society. Lindsay was much influenced by these chants, which he greatly admired. He also admired dancing, and enjoyed occasions when he was able to read his poems as a kind of musical backing for the footwork or performance of a particular dancer, such as Ruth Lovett.

Once when Bob Dylan was asked, are you a poet or are you a singer? he replied, I am a dancer. Vachel Lindsay would have approved of this answer. Consider whether *Daniel* could be danced to. Try it out, splitting up into a group who chant, as music, and a group who dance to the chant. Think of the rhythm more than the meaning. Go with the flow. Feel the poem in your legs. Let it make you move. Your body can be deeply moved by a poem as much as your heart or your mind. The poem may come to life through you in the way you walk as well as the way you think or feel. A poem is a rhythm, and a rhythm can be a bodily thing.

Factory Windows Are Always Broken

Many of Vachel Lindsay's shorter poems, which are not usually his best, were written to go with his own drawings. The link between picture and word, as in Egyptian hieroglyphics, interested Lindsay in the same way as the link between dance step and word. This short poem illustrates his social conscience in a vivid pair of images – the despised factory, with its broken windows, and the revered chapel, with its clean stained-glass ones. What do you think? Could this poem be supplemented, or replaced, by a drawing? Try illustrating it for yourself, and see what has to be left out. What about line eight, for example? Could you draw that? Notice the reference to 'Denmark' near the end, and the echo here of Shakespeare's play *Hamlet*. How does this reference help?

D H Lawrence

The novelist and poet D H Lawrence died in 1930, long before the Second World War, and yet his poetry is in many ways more alive and relevant now than it was when he wrote it. Some poets acquire a quick reputation, and are understood and widely read during their own lifetimes; others take time to break through. Lawrence belongs to this second class, largely because his best verse, like his later prose, took many risks both in form and subject matter, and wasn't afraid to shock and to provoke thought. Most of the poems by Lawrence in this book are from a late collection called *Pansies*, and I cannot do better than quote his own introduction:

> This little bunch of fragments is offered as a bunch of *pensees*, anglice pansies; a handful of thoughts. Or, if you will have the other derivation of pansy, from *panser*, to dress or soothe a wound; these are my tender administrations to the mental and emotional wounds we suffer from...... Each little piece is a thought; not a bare idea or an opinion or a didactic statement, but a true thought, which comes as much from the heart and the genitals as from the head.

Thoughts to dress a wound. Not a bad definition of one kind of poetry. Lawrence suffered (and finally died) from tuberculosis, and he was kept out of the First World War by ill health; but he experienced a good deal of prejudice in that war through his marriage to a German woman, and a good deal more after the war through his frank writing about sex. In many ways, Lawrence paid the penalty for being 'ahead of his time', and I sometimes like to imagine him as an old man in his nineties, watching with a benevolent eye some of the freedoms of the 1970s which he'd fought for in the 1920s. As it was, he died at the age of forty-five, before he was fully recognized.

Work

There is no point in work
unless it absorbs you
like an absorbing game.

If it doesn't absorb you
if it's never any fun,
don't do it.

When a man goes out into his work
he is alive like a tree in spring,
he is living, not merely working.

When the Hindus weave thin wool into long, long
    lengths of stuff
with their thin dark hands and their wide dark eyes and
    their still souls absorbed
they are like slender trees putting forth leaves, a long
    white web of living leaf,
the tissue they weave,
and they clothe themselves in white as a tree clothes
    itself in its own foliage.

As with cloth, so with houses, ships, shoes, wagons or
    cups or loaves
men might put them forth as a snail its shell, as a bird
    that leans
its breast against its nest, to make it round,
as the turnip models his round root, as the bush makes
    flowers and gooseberries,
putting them forth, not manufacturing them,
and cities might be as once they were, bowers grown out
    from the busy bodies of people.

And so it will be again, men will smash the machines.

At last, for the sake of clothing himself in his own
    leaf-like cloth
tissued from his life,
and dwelling in his own bowery house, like a beaver's
    nibbled mansion
and drinking from cups that came off his fingers like
    flowers off their five-fold stem,
he will cancel the machines we have got.

Self-Pity

I never saw a wild thing
sorry for itself.
A small bird will drop frozen dead from a bough
without ever having felt sorry for itself.

Elemental

Why don't people leave off being lovable
or thinking they are lovable, or wanting to be lovable,
and be a bit elemental instead?

Since man is made up of the elements
fire, and rain, and air, and live loam
and none of these is lovable
but elemental,
man is lop-sided on the side of the angels.

I wish men would get back their balance among the
    elements
and be a bit more fiery, as incapable of telling lies
as fire is.

I wish they'd be true to their own variation, as water is,
which goes through all the stages of steam and stream
    and ice
without losing its head.

I am sick of lovable people,
somehow they are a lie.

Willy Wet-Leg

I can't stand Willy wet-leg,
can't stand him at any price.
He's resigned, and when you hit him
he lets you hit him twice.

Noble

I know I am noble with the nobility of the sun.
A certain peace, a certain grace.
I would say the same if I were a chaffinch or tree.

No! Mr Lawrence!

No, Mr Lawrence, it's not like that!
I don't mind telling you
I know a thing or two about love,
Perhaps more than you do.

And what I know is that you make it
Too nice, too beautiful.
It's not like that, you know; you fake it.
It's really rather dull.

Money-Madness

Money is our madness, our vast collective madness.

And of course, if the multitude is mad
the individual carries his own grain of insanity around
      with him.

I doubt if any man living hands out a pound note
      without a pang;
and a real tremor, if he hands out a ten-pound note.

We quail, money makes us quail.
It has got us down, we grovel before it in strange terror.
And no wonder, for money has a fearful cruel power
      among men.

But it is not money we are so terrified of,
it is the collective money-madness of mankind.
For mankind says with one voice: How much is he
      worth?
Has he no money? Then let him eat dirt, and go cold. –

And if I have no money, they will give me a little bread
so I do not die,
but they will make me eat dirt with it.
I shall have to eat dirt, I shall have to eat dirt
if I have no money.

It is that that I am frightened of.
And that fear can become a delirium.
It is fear of my money-mad fellow-men.

We must have some money
to save us from eating dirt.

And this is all wrong.

Bread should be free,
shelter should be free,
fire should be free
to all and anybody, all and anybody, all over the world.

We must regain our sanity about money
before we start killing one another about it.
It's one thing or the other.

The Grudge of the Old

The old ones want to be young, and they aren't young,
and it rankles, they ache when they see the young,
and they can't help wanting to spite it on them
    venomously.

The old ones say to themselves: We are not going to be
    old,
we are not going to make way, we are not going to die,
we are going to stay on and on and on and on and on
and make the young look after us
till they are old. We are stronger than the young.
We have more energy, and our grip on life is harder.
Let us triumph, and let the young be listless
with their puny youth.
We are younger even now than the young, we can put
    their youth in abeyance.

And it is true.
And they do it.
And so it goes on.

To Women, as far as I'm Concerned

The feelings I don't have I don't have.
The feelings I don't have, I won't say I have.
The feelings you say you have, you don't have.
The feelings you would like us both to have, we neither
of us have.
The feelings people ought to have, they never have.
If people say they've got feelings, you may be pretty
sure they haven't got them.

So if you want either of us to feel anything at all
you'd better abandon all idea of feelings altogether.

Being Alive

The only reason for living is being fully alive;
and you can't be fully alive if you are crushed by secret
    fear,
and bullied with the threat: Get money, or eat dirt! –
and forced to do a thousand mean things meaner than
    your nature,
and forced to clutch on to possessions in the hope they'll
    make you feel safe,
and forced to watch everyone that comes near you, lest
    they've come to do you down.

Without a bit of common trust in one another, we can't
    live.
In the end, we go insane.
It is the penalty of fear and meanness, being meaner
    than our natures are.

To be alive, you've got to feel a generous flow,
and under a competitive system that is impossible,
    really.
The world is waiting for a new great movement of
    generosity,
or for a great wave of death.
We must change the system, and make living free to all
    men,
or we must see men die, and then die ourselves.

What is Man Without an Income?

What is man without an income?
– Well, let him get on the dole!

Dole, dole, dole,
hole, hole, hole
soul, soul, soul –

What is man without an income?
Answer without a rigmarole.

On the dole, dole, dole
he's a hole, hole hole
in the nation's pocket.

– Now then, you leave a man's misfortunes alone!

He's got a soul, soul, soul
but the coal, coal, coal
on the whole, whole, whole
doesn't pay,
so the dole, dole, dole's
the only way.

And on the dole, dole, dole
a man's a hole, hole, hole
in the nation's pocket,
and his soul, soul, soul
won't stop a hole, hole, hole
though his ashes might.

Immortal Caesar dead and turned to clay
would stop a hole to keep the wind away.

But a man without a job
isn't even as good as a gob
of clay.

Body and soul
he's just a hole
down which the nation's resources roll
away.

Prestige

I never met a single
middle-class person whose
nerves didn't tighten against me
as if they'd got something to lose.

Though what it was, you can ask me:
some mysterious sort of prestige
that was nothing to me; though they always
seemed to think I was laying it siege.

It was something I never could fathom,
that mysterious prestige which they all
seemed to think they'd got, like a halo
around them, an invisible wall.

If you were willing to see it
they were only too eager to grant
you a similar glory, since you'd risen
to their levels, my holy aunt!

But never, no never could I see it,
and so I could never feel
the proper unction about it,
and it worried me a good deal.

For years and years it bothered me
that I couldn't feel one of them,
till at last I saw the reason:
they were just a bloody sham.

As far as any superiority
or halo or prestige went
they were just a bloody collective fraud,
that was what their *Ahem!* meant.

Their superiority was meanness,
they were cunning about the goods
and sly with a lot of after-thought,
and they put it over us, the duds!

And I'd let myself be swindled
half believing 'em, till one day
I suddenly said: I've finished!
My God, let me get away!

The Jeune Fille

Oh the innocent girl
in her maiden teens
knows perfectly well
what everything means.

If she didn't, she oughter;
it's a silly shame
to pretend that your daughter
is a blank at the game.

Anyhow she despises
your fool pretence
that she's just a sheep
and can't see through the fence.

Oh every lass
should hear all the rough words
and laugh, let them pass;
and be used to the turds

as well as the grass;
and know that she's got
in herself a small treasure
that may yet give a lot

of genuine pleasure
to a decent man;
and beware and take care
of it while she can.

If she never knows
what is her treasure,
she grows and throws
it away, and you measure

the folly of that
from her subsequent woes.
Oh the innocent maid,
when she knows what's what

from the top of her head
to the tips of her toes
is more innocent far
than the blank-it-out girl

who gets into the car
and just fills you with hell.

Conundrums

Tell me a word
that you've often heard,
yet it makes you squint
if you see it in print!

Tell me a thing
that you've often seen,
yet if put in a book
it makes you turn green!

Tell me a thing
that you often do,
which described in a story
shocks you through and through!

Tell me what's wrong
with words or with you
that you don't mind the thing
yet the name is taboo.

Baby Tortoise

You know what it is to be born alone,
Baby tortoise!

The first day to heave your feet little by little from the
    shell,
Not yet awake,
And remain lapsed on earth,
Not quite alive.

A tiny, fragile, half-animate bean.

To open your tiny beak-mouth, that looks as if it would
    never open,
Like some iron door;
To lift the upper hawk-beak from the lower base
And reach your skinny little neck
And take your first bite at some dim bit of herbage,
Alone, small insect,
Tiny bright-eye,
Slow one.

To take your first solitary bite
And move on your slow, solitary hunt.
Your bright, dark little eye,
Your eye of a dark disturbed night,
Under its slow lid, tiny baby tortoise,
So indomitable.

No one ever heard you complain.

You draw your head forward, slowly, from your little
    wimple
And set forward, slow-dragging, on your four-pinned
    toes,
Rowing slowly forward.
Whither away, small bird?
Rather like a baby working its limbs,
Except that you make slow, ageless progress
And a baby makes none.
The touch of sun excites you,
And the long ages, and the lingering chill
Make you pause to yawn,
Opening your impervious mouth,
Suddenly beak-shaped, and very wide, like some
    suddenly gaping pincers;
Soft red tongue, and hard thin gums,
Then close the wedge of your little mountain front,
Your face, baby tortoise.

Do you wonder at the world, as slowly you turn your
    head in its wimple
And look with laconic, black eyes?
Or is sleep coming over you again,
The non-life?

You are so hard to wake.

Are you able to wonder?
Or is it just your indomitable will and pride of the first
    life
Looking round
And slowly pitching itself against the inertia
Which had seemed invincible?

The vast inanimate,
And the fine brilliance of your so tiny eye,
Challenger.

Nay, tiny shell-bird,
What a huge vast inanimate it is, that you must row
        against,
What an incalculable inertia.

Challenger,
Little Ulysses, fore-runner,
No bigger than my thumb-nail,
Buon viaggio.

All animate creation on your shoulder,
Set forth, little Titan, under your battle-shield.

The ponderous, preponderate,
Inanimate universe;
And you are slowly moving, pioneer, you alone.

How vivid your travelling seems now, in the troubled
        sunshine,
Stoic, Ulyssean atom;
Suddenly hasty, reckless, on high toes.

Voiceless little bird,
Resting your head half out of your wimple
In the slow dignity of your eternal pause.
Alone, with no sense of being alone,
And hence six times more solitary;
Fulfilled of the slow passion of pitching through
        immemorial ages
Your little round house in the midst of chaos.

Over the garden earth,
Small bird,
Over the edge of all things.

Traveller,
With your tail tucked a little on one side
Like a gentleman in a long-skirted coat.

All life carried on your shoulder,
Invincible fore-runner.

The Mosquito

When did you start your tricks,
Monsieur?

What do you stand on such high legs for?
Why this length of shredded shank,
You exaltation?

Is it so that you shall lift your centre of gravity upwards
And weigh no more than air as you alight upon me,
Stand upon me weightless, you phantom?

I heard a woman call you the Winged Victory
In sluggish Venice.
You turn your head towards your tail, and smile.

How can you put so much devilry
Into that translucent phantom shred
Of a frail corpus?

Queer, with your thin wings and your streaming legs,
How you sail like a heron, or a dull clot of air,
A nothingness.

Yet what an aura surrounds you;
Your evil little aura, prowling, and casting a numbness
    on my mind.

That is your trick, your bit of filthy magic:
Invisibility, and the anaesthetic power
To deaden my attention in your direction.

But I know your game now, streaky sorcerer.
Queer, how you stalk and prowl the air
In circles and evasions, enveloping me,
Ghoul on wings
Winged Victory.

Settle, and stand on long thin shanks
Eyeing me sideways, and cunningly conscious that I am
    aware,
You speck.

I hate the way you lurch off sideways into air
Having read my thoughts against you.

Come then, let us play at unawares,
And see who wins in this sly game of bluff.
Man or mosquito.

You don't know that I exist, and I don't know that you
    exist.
Now then!

It is your trump,
It is your hateful little trump,
You pointed fiend,
Which shakes my sudden blood to hatred of you:
It is your small, high, hateful bugle in my ear.

Why do you do it?
Surely it is bad policy.

They say you can't help it.

If that is so, then I believe a little in Providence
        protecting the innocent.
But it sounds so amazingly like a slogan,
A yell of triumph as you snatch my scalp.

Blood, red blood
Super-magical
Forbidden liquor.

I behold you stand
For a second enspasmed in oblivion.
Obscenely ecstasied
Sucking live blood,
My blood.

Such silence, such suspended transport,
Such gorging,
Such obscenity of trespass.

You stagger
As well as you may.
Only your accursed hairy frailty,
Your own imponderable weightlessness
Saves you, wafts you away on the very draught my
    anger makes in its snatching.

Away with a pæan of derision,
You winged blood-drop.

Can I not overtake you?
Are you one too many for me,
Winged Victory?
Am I not mosquito enough to out-mosquito you?

Queer, what a big stain my sucked blood makes
Beside the infinitesimal faint smear of you!
Queer, what a dim dark smudge you have disappeared
    into!

Siracusa.

Notes

Work

Think about what Lawrence really means. Is he saying that we ought to be lazy whenever we're bored? I don't think so. Is he saying that all machines are bad? I don't think he's saying that either. Heart pacemakers are a good thing – aren't they? Think about it for yourself. Are there any arguments against medical machines? Do they ever prolong life unnecessarily, cruelly? Do they create a climate where people don't try hard enough to keep healthy? Then what about more controversial machines like motorcars, television sets? There are people who wish that neither of these had been invented, but I suspect most of us feel they bring great benefits and make life more fulfilling. But what about nuclear weapons? Do you think that nuclear energy makes life better? Try and make your own private list of good and bad machines. Then have a discussion and compare your lists. Lawrence wants you to think. His poem is putting a point of view, and it's meant to stimulate your own desire to think (and feel by thinking) for yourselves.

Self-Pity

This is a very short, plain claim. The first sentence is a personal statement, and one we can't easily challenge. But what about the second sentence? Lawrence is passing from his own particular experience to a generalization based upon it. Is he allowed to do this? Of course he is. But is what he is saying true? The point is that Lawrence wants us, as human beings, to be more tough, and not complain so much, and he hopes that the dying fledgling will be an example and an inspiration. So it does matter if what he is saying is true. But it isn't exactly a scientific statement like: metals don't float – so we can't check it by experiment. We have to make a sort of imaginative – and then a sort of moral – leap. This is often demanded of us by the rhetoric of poems. They work like evangelists, or politicians. They demand our allegiance. But we ought to stop and think before we give it. Then, if we choose to, we should give it totally.

Elemental

This is a poem against bothering too much to be thought nice. It's more important, Lawrence tells us, to be yourself. Well, is it? Aren't there dangers in just giving free rein to your own impulses and moods? What if you feel like kicking somebody? Yes: but what if you feel like helping an old lady across the road, and then hang back because you're shy or because your friends might think you're soppy? Try and write down the balance between acting without stopping to think and working out all your moves in your head before you make them. List examples.

Willy Wet-Leg

This is a sort of contradiction of the Christian ethic about always turning the other cheek. List some instances where it would be wrong to hit back straightaway. Try writing a four-line poem called BILLY BASH-BACK about someone who always retaliates at the slightest provocation.

Noble

Lawrence often argues for the superior dignity of the natural world. He sees animals and plants – even elemental forces – as being there to be copied and learned from. Our human glory lies in recognizing a kinship with the world round about us, not in forcing its denizens and powers to be subject to our will. Is this romantic and beautiful, or just plain eccentric? What about the nobility of the common cold virus, or the deadly nightshade?

No! Mr Lawrence!

This poem does exactly what I have been doing in my notes. It imagines an objection to what the poet himself is saying. So let's follow his own gentle hint. Let's put in a good word for love, the way some of the poems not printed here do. Write down three things about love that make it unique and wonderful. Make them funny, if you like – for example: love makes me forget what a nice game Patience is – or make them serious.

Money-Madness

You might call this a poem against the whole capitalist system. But it's not exactly a Marxist poem. In fact, there is nothing really political about it at all. It's a poem of anger and compassion, not of reasoned argument. Would it have been better as an essay, or a political speech? Or does the feeling require this direct, pithy expression rather than a more stretched-out one? Try writing your own poem on a similar subject: war-madness, perhaps.

The Grudge of the Old

Is it really true that old people try to keep back the advancement of the young, as Lawrence suggests? Probably not, or at least not always. Some old people do become crotchety and bigoted, certainly. Nevertheless, it could be said that energy of repression is a useful antidote to listlessness of submission. Old people who tend to be weak, and simply let things go, might learn from old people who cling on and stick to their guns. Try writing a poem called The Sadness of the Old, about feeling out of everything. Then try writing another poem called The Grudge of the Young, about feeling excluded and kept back.

To Women, as far as I'm Concerned

This poem might win Lawrence the title of Male Chauvinist Pig. But at least it's honest. Or is it? Isn't there any place for romance at all in the world? Is it a man's view to want everything to be black and white, and practical? Perhaps the title is a clue here. It seems to admit that Lawrence may be regarding himself as an unusual case. Then again, perhaps it's the voice of a passing mood. Isn't the poem really like a snatch of overheard argument, ripped out of context? Try writing a woman's speech to go before, and then another to come after, this outburst. You may find you're on the edge of writing a little verse play between two characters who can't get on with each other.

Being Alive

This is a dispersed, rhetorical poem that sums up a lot of Lawrence's views. It has the garrulous quality of someone elaborating a point over a pint in a pub. He goes on a bit, but the alcohol has loosened his tongue and he brings out some real feelings – too many, you may think. But isn't there sometimes a place for urgency without logic? Why not write a very neutral poem describing what an imaginary listener might see while an imaginary speaker like the one in the poem was talking: a view through a window, perhaps; a crowd in a bar; bottles, a girl serving ale; the face of a man out of work, flushed with drink, who wants society to change.

What is Man Without an Income?

This one might go to a tune, with some music. If you play the guitar – or sing – you might like to get together with one or two others in the class and try composing a song, using some or all of

Lawrence's words. The quotation about Julius Caesar from Shakespeare's *Hamlet* might be hard to fit in, but do your best.

Prestige

Do you feel the same as Lawrence about middle-class people? What makes you middle class, anyway? Are *you* middle class? Is your teacher? Who isn't middle class? Mick Jagger? The Queen? Mrs Thatcher? Is being middle class below being famous and above being ordinary? Or doesn't it work like that? How does it work? Are middle-class people the enemy? Or do middle-class people have to protect themselves against some other enemy? If so, who? Mr Benn? The Russians? Black people? Or isn't there a class war any more? Or do we have more important wars on our plate?

The Jeune Fille

Giving this poem a French title rather draws our attention to what – in Lawrence's day – might have been thought its 'naughty' subject matter. Anything to do with France was once thought to be erotic, hence expressions like 'French letter' for contraceptive. Sex education is now commonplace, but it wasn't always. Lawrence is arguing – as he often does – that there is nothing disgusting about knowing the way your own body works. What about the end of this poem, though? Is it clear what it means? Is Lawrence suggesting that sexual ignorance leads to fast driving, or to leading boys on in quiet places to go so far and no further?

Conundrums

Lawrence is thinking here about sex, and the so-called 'four letter' words. But he might easily not be. Think of some non-sexual words that make you squirm when you see them in print: snot, perhaps. Then think of non-sexual activities that none of us mind but that we disguise in evasive language. What about when we eat pig and want to call it pork; or when the Mafia want to kill someone and talk of taking out a contract; or when we call a hydrogen bomb a nuclear deterrent? Lawrence has often been accused of being a dirty – or sex-obsessed – writer, but what he says about sex can often be transferred to some other area.

Baby Tortoise

Lawrence is at his best as a poet when he writes about animals, and the baby tortoise here is conjured up with great faithfulness and affection. It's a masterpiece of accurate and vivid description. The feeling of tenderness for the little strange creature is what finally makes the poem more than just a string of clever comparisons. Try taking some other unusual animal – or insect or fish – and making it seem charming and lovable the way Lawrence does. What about a warthog or a tadpole?

The Mosquito

This is a much less affectionate poem. The mosquito is viewed with a quizzical antagonism. It's a swatter's eye view of this tiny bloodsucker. Notice the skill with which Lawrence evokes his enemy, though. Despite the enormous disparity in scale between human and mosquito, the poet's zoom lens brings him close enough to draw a very exact portrait. Why not try the same thing in reverse? How about a worm's eye view of an elephant trampling through a garden? A small antagonist viewing a large opponent: the plankton about to be swallowed by the whale. Then try working out the mosquito's reply to Lawrence. A little winged warrior trying to capture the food essential to its life.

Stevie Smith

Stevie Smith worked for many years as a secretary in London, and a good deal of her private life was taken up in caring for an elderly aunt, with whom she shared a house in Palmer's Green. Her very eccentric and individual tone of voice was slow to make its mark and, although she published poems and a novel in the 1930s, it wasn't until she was well into middle age that her poetry really began to be widely recognized. This was partly due to her great – and apparently artless – skill as a public performer, which thrived on the platform variety of the 1960s. A younger generation took her up as a natural English character, a survivor of the great Edwardian age in which she had grown up as a child. The very modernity of Stevie Smith's verse seemed to come from its old-fashioned quality: it seemed that her doggerel style, and Edward Lear-like drawings, were a way of poking fun at the pretentiousness of all the traditional poets in the school anthologies. Nowadays we can see her as a pioneer feminist – unconscious or not – as a good fairy obsessed with death, or as a believing Christian at perpetual odds with the rites of her faith. Most of all we can see her as a direct, funny writer free from all bookishness, and with a style so near to rubbish that only genius could have drawn the hair's-breadth line of separation.

Alfred the Great

Honour and magnify this man of men
Who keeps a wife and seven children on £2 10
Paid weekly in an envelope
And yet he never has abandoned hope.

Correspondence between Mr Harrison in Newcastle and Mr Sholto Peach Harrison in Hull

Sholto Peach Harrison you are no son of mine
And do you think I bred you up to cross the River Tyne
And do you think I bred you up (and mother says the
     same)
And do you think I bred you up to live a life of shame
To live a life of shame my boy as you are thinking to

Down south in Kingston-upon-Hull a traveller in glue?
Come back my bonny boy nor break your father's heart
Come back and marry Lady Susan Smart
She has a mint in Anglo-Persian oil
And Sholto never more need think of toil.

You are an old and evil man my father
I tell you frankly Sholto had much rather
Travel in glue unrecompensed unwed
Than go to church with oily Sue and afterwards to bed.

O Happy Dogs of England

O happy dogs of England
Bark well as well you may
If you lived anywhere else
You would not be so gay.

O happy dogs of England
Bark well at errand boys
If you lived anywhere else
You would not be allowed to make such an infernal
    noise.

Croft

Aloft,
In the loft,
Sits Croft;
He is soft.

The River God

I may be smelly and I may be old,
Rough in my pebbles, reedy in my pools,
But where my fish float by I bless their swimming
And I like the people to bathe in me, especially women.
But I can drown the fools
Who bathe too close to the weir, contrary to rules.
And they take a long time drowning
As I throw them up now and then in a spirit of
     clowning.
Hi yih, yippity-yap, merrily I flow,
O I may be an old foul river but I have plenty of go.
Once there was a lady who was too bold
She bathed in me by the tall black cliff where the water
     runs cold,
So I brought her down here
To be my beautiful dear.
Oh will she stay with me will she stay
This beautiful lady, or will she go away?
She lies in my beautiful deep river bed with many a
     weed

To hold her, and many a waving reed.
Oh who would guess what a beautiful white face lies
    there
Waiting for me to smooth and wash away the fear
She looks at me with. Hi yih, do not let her
Go. There is no one on earth who does not forget her
Now. They say I am a foolish old smelly river
But they do not know of my wide original bed
Where the lady waits, with her golden sleepy head.
If she wishes to go I will not forgive her.

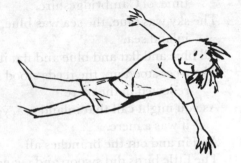

Drugs Made Pauline Vague

Drugs made Pauline vague.
She sat one day at the breakfast table
Fingering in a baffled way
The fronds of the maidenhair plant.

Was it the salt you were looking for dear?
Said Dulcie, exchanging a glance with the Brigadier.

Chuff chuff Pauline what's the matter?
Said the Brigadier to his wife
Who did not even notice
What a handsome couple they made.

The Engine Drain

A Fenland Memory

It was the mighty Engine Drain, the Engine Drain, the
    Engine Drain,
Down which the water went, the water went, the
    mighty waters of the inland sea.
But still in memory I see, the inland sea, the inland sea
That did reflect the summer sky, when it was summer
    time, of Cambridgeshire.
The sky was blue, the sea was blue, the inland sea, the
    inland sea,
All blue and flat and blue and flat it lay for all to see.
The trees stood up, the reeds stood too, and were
    reflected in the mere
As you might call that inland sea, you might have said
    it was a mere.
And in and out the branches all
The little birds did swoop and swing
Did swoop and swing and call
And oh it was a pretty thing to see them swoop and
    swing.
Oh ho the inland sea, the inland sea, the mighty mere
    that moved so prettily.

When winter came the water rose,
And rose and rose and rose and rose
And all about the cottage floors
It flowed and rose and flowed and rose
Till in their beds at night you'd see
Quite half afloat the midnight peasantry
That got their living hardily
And died of ripe old age rheumatically,

Oh it was quite surprising how
They'd live to ripe old age rheumatically.
It was because they early learnt
To put their boots on properly
While still in bed, while still in bed.
They learnt to put their boots on properly
Afloat in bed upon the inland sea.

And now I do remember how
Looking from shallow banks below
You'd see the little water-snakes
A-swimming to and fro,
So many little water-snakes
Careering round about
No man might stand to count them there
Careering in the pretty mere.

Oh it was merry in that day
To see the water-fowl play
Upon the inland sea,
Chip-chopping in the sea;
Or see them ride the water-race
In winter, till the winds in chase
Drove them ashore. Oh ho the wind upon the mere
It wound the waves in heaps and tossed the spray
That was half froze, upon the darkening day
Whipping the waters up till you might see
A mile away the whitecaps of the inland sea,
The whitecaps of the mere.

Ah me alas the day is past, is past and long ago
And no man living now may say he saw the waters flow,
All all are gone, the Engine Drain
Has took them to the cruel salt sea

And what is left behind?
A fertile flat and farming land,
A profitable farming land
Is what is left behind,
It took some time, as you might guess,
But not so long as you would guess,
A day or two, or two or three,
To take these waters to the sea
To take them to the Wash.

Why was it called the Engine Drain, the Engine Drain,
    the Engine Drain?
It was because the others were,
The other drains of Cambridgeshire,
Controlled by air, by windmills blowing there.
But oh this Engine was a force, a mighty engineering
    force,
It took the waters of the mere and brought them to the
    Wash,
It took them, did the Engine Drain, these waters of the
    inland sea,
And droppt 'em in the cruel salt sea,
The cruel salt sea.

The Hostage

You hang at dawn, they said,
You've done nothing wrong but at dawn you will be
    hung.
You'll pass tonight in this cell
With Father Whatshisname. He'll look after you well.

There were two truckle beds in the room, on one sat
    Father W,
Reclining against a bolster. The lady sat on the other.

I should like you to hear my confession, Father, I'm not
    of your persuasion
I'm a member of the Church of England, but on this
    occasion
I should like to talk to you, if you'll allow, nothing
    more,
Just a talk, not really a confession, but my heart is sore.
No, it's not that I have to die, that's the trouble, I've
    always wanted to
But it seems so despondent you know, ungracious too,

She sighed. Daughter, proceed,
Said the Father. I am here at your need.

Even as a child, said the lady, I recall in my pram
Wishing it was over and done with. Oh I am
Already at fault. Wonderful how 'bright' they keep,
I'd say of the other children, quite without rancour,
    then turn again to sleep.
Yet life is so beautiful. Oh the scenery.
Have you ever seen the sun getting up in the greenery

Of a summer day, in Norfolk say,
And the mild farm animals lumbering in the thistles.
Presently the Five-Thirty Milk in the station whistles,
You can hear the clank of the cans. In the wood
Trees dip to the stream, the fish rise up for food,
Shap, the old fly's caught. Et cetera. Oh it's busy,
Life bustles in the country, you know; it should be easy.

But I was outside of it, looking, finding no place,
No excuse at all for my distant wandering face.

When I came to London West-Eight, it was much the
        same
Oh the beautiful faces of others in the falling rain,
In the buses, no fuss there, no question they weren't at
        home,
Oh why should it only be I that was sent to roam?
I tell you, Father, I trod out the troughs of despair,
I'd rush out of doors in a fit, hurry, anywhere,
Kiss in my mind the darlings, beg them to stop ...
Till the wind came up hard and blew my beauties off.
The wind blew hard. I snuffed it up and liked it,
Oh yes I liked it, that was the worst of it.

Of course I never dared form any close acquaintance.
Marriage? Out of the question. Well for instance
It might be infectious, this malaise of mine (an
        excuse?). Spread
That? I'd rather be dead.
But will the Lord forgive me? Is it wrong?
Will He forgive me do you think for not minding being
        hung,

Being glad it will soon be over,
Hoping he isn't the Ruler, the busy Lover,
Wishing to wake again, if I must at all,
As a vegetable leaning against a quiet wall,
Or an old stone, so old it was here before Man,
Or a flash in the fire that split our world from the sun?

I find nothing to instruct me in this in Holy Writ,
Said Father W, only, Remember life not to cling to it.

Well I don't you know, said the lady, then aware of
     something comical
Shot him a look that made him feel uncomfortable
Until he remembered she came from the British Isles,
Oh, he said, I've heard that's a place where nobody
     smiles.
But they do, said the lady, who loved her country, they
     laugh like anything
There is no one on earth who laughs so much about
     everything.

Well I see, said the Father, the case is complicated,
I will pray for you, Daughter, as I pray for all created
Meanwhile, since you want to die and have to, you may
go on feeling elated.

The Past

People who are always praising the past
And especially the times of faith as best
Ought to go and live in the Middle Ages
And be burnt at the stake as witches and sages.

Emily writes such a good letter

Mabel was married last week
So now only Tom left

The doctor didn't like Arthur's cough
I have been in bed since Easter

A touch of the old trouble

I am downstairs today
As I write this
I can hear Arthur roaming overhead

He loves to roam
Thank heavens he has plenty of space to roam in

We have seven bedrooms
And an annexe

Which leaves a flat for the chauffeur and his wife

We have much to be thankful for

The new vicar came yesterday
People say he brings a breath of fresh air

He leaves me cold
I do not think he is a gentleman

Yes, I remember Maurice very well
Fancy getting married at his age
She must be a fool

You knew May had moved?
Since Edward died she has been much alone

It was cancer

No, I know nothing of Maud
I never wish to hear her name again
In my opinion Maud
Is an evil woman

Our char has left
And a good riddance too
Wages are very high in Tonbridge

Write and tell me how you are, dear,
And the girls,
Phoebe and Rose
They must be a great comfort to you
Phoebe and Rose.

The Grange

Oh there hasn't been much change
At the Grange,

Of course the blackberries growing closer
Make getting in a bit of a poser,
But there hasn't been much change
At the Grange.

Old Sir Prior died,
They say on the point of leaving for the seaside,
They never found the body, which seemed odd to some
(Not me, seeing as what I seen the butler done.)

Oh there hasn't been much change
At the Grange.

The governess 'as got it now,
Miss Ursy 'aving moved down to the Green Cow –

Proper done out of 'er rights, she was, a b shame.
And what's that the governess pushes round at nights in
    the old pram?

Oh there hasn't been much change
At the Grange.

The shops leave supplies at the gate now, meat,
    groceries,
Mostly old tinned stuff you know from McInnes's,
They wouldn't go up to the door,
Not after what happened to Fred's pa.

Oh there hasn't been much change
At the Grange.

Parssing there early this morning, cor lummy,
I'ears a whistling sound coming from the old chimney,
Whistling it was fit to bust and not a note wrong,
The old pot, whistling The Death of Nelson.

No there hasn't been much change
At the Grange,

But few goes that way somehow,
Not now.

STEVIE SMITH

The Galloping Cat

Oh I am a cat that likes to
Gallop about doing good
So
One day when I was
Galloping about doing good, I saw
A Figure in the path; I said:
Get off! (Be-
cause
I am a cat that likes to
Gallop about doing good)
But he did not move, instead
He raised his hand as if
To land me a cuff
So I made to dodge so as to
Prevent him bringing it orf,
Un-for-tune-ately I slid
On a banana skin
Some Ass had left instead
Of putting in the bin. So
His hand caught me on the cheek
I tried
To lay his arm open from wrist to elbow
With my sharp teeth
Because I am
A cat that likes to gallop about doing good.
Would you believe it?
He wasn't there
My teeth met nothing but air,
But a Voice said: Poor cat,
(Meaning me) and a soft stroke
Came on me head
Since when
I have been bald.

66

I regard myself as
A martyr to doing good.
Also I heard a swoosh
As of wings, and saw
A halo shining at the height of
Mrs Gubbins's backyard fence,
So I thought: What's the good
Of galloping about doing good
When angels stand in the path
And do not do as they should
Such as having an arm to be bitten off
All the same I
Intend to go on being
A cat that likes to
Gallop about doing good
So
Now with my bald head I go,
Chopping the untidy flowers down, to and fro,
An' scooping up the grass to show
Underneath
The cinder path of wrath
Ha ha ha ha, ho,
Angels aren't the only ones who do not know
What's what and that
Galloping about doing good
Is a full-time job
That needs
An experienced eye of earthly
Sharpness, worth I dare say
(If you'll forgive a personal note)
A good deal more
Than all that skyey stuff
Of angels that make so bold as
To pity a cat like me that
Gallops about doing good.

Notes

Alfred the Great

Notice how the second line deflates the grand tone of the first line. £2 10 is £2.50 in present-day money, but the real value is hard to assess. Not that it matters. The point is that the man in the poem is on a very low wage. I said the second line 'deflates' the grand tone; but does it? Isn't Stevie Smith really arguing that this working-class Alfred is just as deserving of honour as the famous English king who burnt the cakes? Try a short poem yourself in praise of a poorly paid nurse, or someone on the dole. See if you can give it the same pithy oddity as Stevie Smith does.

Correspondence between Mr Harrison in Newcastle and Mr Sholto Peach Harrison in Hull

Couplet rhyming – AA – and variation between longer, even lines and shorter ones towards the end. You might like to try counting up the number of syllables in each line. Shol. to. Peach. Har. ris. on. you. are. no. son. of. mine. (12) And. do. you. think. I. bred. you. up. to. cross. the. riv. er. Tyne. (14) . . . and so on. The whole poem should be read with a North Country accent. It's really a dialogue in two parts, as the title makes clear. Try it as a short play: the father varying his mood from anger to pleading; the son scornful. Compare this poem with, say, Betjeman's *A Shropshire Lad* (page 76). Which do you like best? Now compare with *Hunter Trials* (page 86). Which do you like best now?

O Happy Dogs of England

Is the poet really talking about dogs? Or is the poem about

people? Is it a poem against political protest? Why can't it just be about dogs? The funny thing is that it seems to be about both dogs *and* political protest. The word 'gay', of course, is used in the sense of 'light-hearted'. Why not try drawing a picture – in Stevie Smith's own style – of the dogs barking? Then draw one in *your* own style.

Croft

Soft here means 'mad'. Is there also a tender suggestion that Croft is 'soft' as a small, vulnerable animal feels soft? Or that he is a soft touch? A few words can mean many ideas. A short poem need not be a simple one. Do you know Charlotte Brontë's novel *Jane Eyre*, where Mr Rochester keeps his mad wife in the attic? Think of 'bats in the belfry', and what that phrase means. Imagine the previous history of Croft, and write down why he was 'aloft, in the loft'. Was he Jewish, hiding from the Nazis? Did he kill someone?

The River God

Do you find this poem sick, or hilariously funny, or subtly tender, or just plain weird? I must say I find it a mixture of all four. Some of the language is very romantic, as in a fairy story, but the tone is grim, and a little bit Grimm, too. Is there a difference? Imagine your own fairy story poem, called *The Road God*, about a motorway spirit who enjoys traffic accidents, and has his own dead angel in an abandoned lay-by.

Drugs Made Pauline Vague

Who are the 'handsome couple'? The brigadier and his wife? And, if so, surely Stevie Smith has to be joking? But why not? Or are they Pauline and the maidenhair plant? Is this a sort of surrealist perception of the way the vegetable girl has an affinity for the virgin flower? Might not the poem seem to suggest both ideas? Is this too clever by half?

The Engine Drain

Some lovely effects of repetition – going on and on, the way little children do. This *is* a sort of childhood memory of an East Anglian landscape that exists no more. Compare it with, say, Betjeman's *Trebetherick* (page 74). That's nostalgia; this is more protest, isn't it? Which do you like best? What about trying to write a poem on a row of old Victorian buildings knocked down by a bulldozer to make way for a skyscraper?

Bulldozer, bulldozer, where have you been?
Knocking down Gothic to build a latrine. ... et cetera.

The Hostage

A sort of 1984 poem which works like a one-act play. Read it with four voices. Four, not three – one for the narrative links. How personal do you think this poem is? How far is Stevie Smith writing about herself? It's certainly a very patriotic poem. Do you think British people – British, not English – laugh more than others? If they – we – do, is that a good thing? Might we not seem frivolous to, say, Germans or Americans? Do women laugh as much as men – or more? Does Stevie Smith seem very female to you? Does it matter?

The Past

Is this an anti-Christian poem? Or is it just against fanaticism? Did they burn 'sages' in the Middle Ages? It certainly helps the rhyme, doesn't it? Or is Stevie Smith saying that witches were often wise women, and that they were burned because they were original, and had new, heretical things to say? When would you like to have lived? Yesterday? Tomorrow? In the Stone Age? What would you like to have lived as? A Queen? A servant girl? An executioner?

Emily writes such a good letter

Notice that there is scarcely any punctuation in this poem. The arrangement of the lines brings out the sense without needing punctuation. Try this effect for yourself, breaking up a letter poem into one phrase or sentence unit per line. Ramble on, putting in proper names and family news. Then imagine yourself as someone else – an old aunt, say, or a younger brother – and try to adapt your way of talking to make your letter sound like them. Do you think Stevie Smith's piece is a poem? If yes, what makes it one? The rhythm? The feel of the character? A sort of underlying sadness?

The Grange

Who do you think is talking here? Someone from a nearby village? A former servant? There's a sinister touch – a sort of Agatha Christie quality, perhaps – and the 'off' tone of the rhymes helps this: closer/poser; shame/pram; lummy/chimney. Admiral Nelson was born in Norfolk, where the poem may be set.

The Galloping Cat

Notice how the short lines, and the way each ends, help to keep the poem rushing forwards. In fact, it gallops, like the cat. Do you like cats? Anyone who does – like myself – is likely to find it easy to see them as doing a lot more good than angels. But what if you like pigeons, or eagles? How serious do you think the poem is? Do we always have to be serious about poems? Can't we just stand back – or get stuck in – and enjoy them for a change?

John Betjeman

Sir John Betjeman, the poet laureate, was knighted for his services to literature, the first poet to receive such an honour, I believe, since the First World War. The poet 'laureate' – meaning crowned with laurel, because this was a Roman mark of distinction – has the job of celebrating royal occasions in verse, and he is appointed by the Queen from a short list of the most outstanding poets of the day. John Betjeman is perhaps the first really popular – in the sense of well-known and best-selling – poet since Rudyard Kipling. A recent survey suggested that he was even better known than the novelist Graham Greene. All this adds up to the picture of someone almost as reverently and affectionately regarded as a Victorian bishop, and, indeed, there *is* something clerical and nineteenth-century about Betjeman.

Part of his fame has arisen from television broadcasting about architecture, in particular the great and often neglected monuments of the Victorians, and he has also written and spoken frequently about such arts as music hall. Not surprisingly, the 1970s saw a number of records appear with Betjeman accompanying settings of his poems in a way demonstrating an excellent ear for musical rhythm, and there have also been films – with his own voice over – in which poems like *Invasion Exercise on the Poultry Farm* are brought to life on screen. These forays into other arts – though more common for younger poets – are rare for someone in Betjeman's generation, and he can be seen in one light as a standard bearer for progress and experiment. This might shock his older readers, who include a broad and very conservative belt of Home County commuters, but there is no doubt that Betjeman has always been willing – as in poems like *In Westminister Abbey* – to attack pomposity just as readily as to hymn the praises of seaside holidays and hearty girls who play tennis.

Trebetherick

We used to picnic where the thrift
    Grew deep and tufted to the edge;
We saw the yellow foam-flakes drift
    In trembling sponges on the ledge
Below us, till the wind would lift
    Them up the cliff and o'er the hedge.
Sand in the sandwiches, wasps in the tea.
Sun on our bathing-dresses heavy with the wet,
Squelch of the bladder-wrack waiting for the sea,
Fleas round the tamarisk, an early cigarette.

From where the coastguard houses stood
    One used to see, below the hill,
The lichened branches of a wood
    In summer silver-cool and still;
And there the Shade of Evil could
    Stretch out at us from Shilla Mill.
Thick with sloe and blackberry, uneven in the light,
Lonely ran the hedge, the heavy meadow was remote,
The oldest part of Cornwall was the wood as black as
    night,
And the pheasant and the rabbit lay torn open at the
    throat.

But when a storm was at its height,
    And feathery slate was black in rain,
And tamarisks were hung with light
    And golden sand was brown again,
Spring tide and blizzard would unite
    And sea came flooding up the lane.
Waves full of treasure then were roaring up the beach,
Ropes round our mackintoshes, waders warm and dry,

We waited for the wreckage to come swirling into reach,
Ralph, Vasey, Alastair, Biddy, John and I.

    Then roller into roller curled
        And thundered down the rocky bay,
    And we were in a water-world
        Of rain and blizzard, sea and spray,
    And one against the other hurled.
        We struggled round to Greenaway.
Blessed be St Enodoc, blessed be the wave,
Blessed be the springy turf, we pray, pray to thee,
Ask for our children all the happy days you gave
To Ralph, Vasey, Alastair, Biddy, John and me.

A Shropshire Lad

N.B – This should be recited with a Midland accent. Captain Webb, the swimmer and a relation of Mary Webb by marriage, was born at Dawley in an industrial district in Salop.

The gas was on in the Institute,[1]
    The flare was up in the gym,
A man was running a mineral line,
    A lass was singing a hymn,
When Captain Webb the Dawley man,
    Captain Webb from Dawley,
Came swimming along in the old canal
    That carried the bricks to Lawley.
        Swimming along –
        Swimming along –
        Swimming along from Severn,
And paying a call at Dawley Bank while swimming
        along to Heaven.

The sun shone low on the railway line
    And over the bricks and stacks,
And in at the upstairs windows
    Of the Dawley houses' backs,
When we saw the ghost of Captain Webb,
    Webb in a water sheeting,
Come dripping along in a bathing dress
    To the Saturday evening meeting.
        Dripping along –
        Dripping along –
        To the Congregational Hall;

[1] "The Institute was radiant with gas." Ch. XIX, *Boyhood* – a novel in verse by Rev E E Bradford, DD.

Dripping and still he rose over the sill and faded away
    in a wall.

There wasn't a man in Oakengates
    That hadn't got hold of the tale,
And over the valley in Ironbridge,
    And round by Coalbrookdale,
How Captain Webb from Dawley,
    Captain Webb from Dawley
Rose rigid and dead from the old canal
    That carries the bricks to Lawley.
      Rigid and dead –
      Rigid and dead –
      To the Saturday congregation,
Paying a call at Dawley Bank on his way to his
    destination.

In Westminster Abbey

Let me take this other glove off
    As the *vox humana* swells,
And the beauteous fields of Eden
    Bask beneath the Abbey bells.
Here, where England's statesmen lie,
Listen to a lady's cry.

Gracious Lord, oh bomb the Germans.
    Spare their women for Thy Sake,
And if that is not too easy.
    We will pardon Thy Mistake.
But, gracious Lord, whate'er shall be,
Don't let anyone bomb me.

Keep our Empire undismembered
   Guide our Forces by Thy Hand,
Gallant blacks from far Jamaica,
   Honduras and Togoland;
Protect them Lord in all their fights,
And, even more, protect the whites.

Think of what our Nation stands for,
   Books from Boots' and country lanes,
Free speech, free passes, class distinction,
   Democracy and proper drains.
Lord, put beneath Thy special care
One-eighty-nine Cadogan Square.

Although dear Lord I am a sinner,
   I have done no major crime;
Now I'll come to Evening Service
   Whensoever I have the time.
So, Lord, reserve for me a crown.
And do not let my shares go down.

I will labour for Thy Kingdom,
   Help our lads to win the war,
Send white feathers to the cowards
   Join the Women's Army Corps,
Then wash the Steps around Thy Throne
In the Eternal Safety Zone.

Now I feel a little better,
   What a treat to hear Thy Word,
Where the bones of leading statesmen,
   Have so often been interr'd.
And now, dear Lord, I cannot wait
Because I have a luncheon date.

On a Portrait of a Deaf Man

The kind old face, the egg-shaped head,
  The tie, discreetly loud,
The loosely fitting shooting clothes,
  A closely fitting shroud.

He liked old City dining-rooms,
  Potatoes in their skin.
But now his mouth is wide to let
  The London clay come in.

He took me on long silent walks
  In country lanes when young,
He knew the name of ev'ry bird
  But not the song it sung.

And when he could not hear me speak
  He smiled and looked so wise
That now I do not like to think
  Of maggots in his eyes.

He liked the rain-washed Cornish air
  And smell of ploughed-up soil,
He liked a landscape big and bare
  And painted it in oil.

But least of all he liked that place
  Which hangs on Highgate Hill
Of soaked Carrara-covered earth
  For Londoners to fill.

He would have liked to say good-bye,
Shake hands with many friends,
In Highgate now his finger-bones
Stick through his finger-ends.

You, God, who treat him thus and thus,
Say 'Save his soul and pray.'
You ask me to believe You and
I only see decay.

from *Summoned by Bells*

Nose! Smell again the early morning smells:
Congealing bacon and my father's pipe;
The after-breakfast freshness out of doors
Where sun had dried the heavy dew and freed
Acres of thyme to scent the links and lawns;
The rotten apples on our shady path
Where blowflies settled upon squashy heaps,
Intent and gorging; at the garden gate
Reek of Solignum on the wooden fence;
Mint round the spring, and fennel in the lane,
And honeysuckle wafted from the hedge;
The Lynams' cess-pool like a body-blow;
Then, clean, medicinal and cold – the sea.
'Breathe in the ozone, John. It's iodine.'
But which is iodine and which is drains?
Salt and hot sun on rubber water-wings . . . .
Home to the luncheon smell of Irish stew
And washing-up stench from the kitchen sink
Because the sump is blocked. The afternoons
Brought coconut smell of gorse; at Mably's farm
Sweet scent of drying cowdung; then the moist
Exhaling of the earth in Shilla woods –
First earth encountered after days of sand.
Evening brought back the gummy smell of toys
And fishy stink of glue and Stickphast paste,
And sleep inside the laundriness of sheets.

Invasion Exercise on the Poultry Farm

Softly croons the radiogram, loudly hoot the owls,
Judy gives the door a slam and goes to feed the fowls.
Marty rolls a Craven A around her ruby lips
And runs her yellow fingers down her corduroyed
      hips,
Shuts her mouth and screws her eyes and puffs her fag
      alight
And hears some most peculiar cries that echo through
      the night.
Ting-a-ling the telephone, to-whit to-whoo the owls,
Judy, Judy, Judy girl, and have you fed the fowls?
No answer as the poultry gate is swinging there ajar.
Boom the bombers overhead, between the clouds a star,
And just outside, among the arks, in a shadowy
      sheltered place
Lie Judy and a paratroop in horrible embrace.
Ting-a-ling the telephone. 'Yes, this is Marty Hayne.'
'Have you seen a paratroop come walking down your
      lane?
He may be on your premises, he may be somewhere
      near,
And if he is report the fact to Major Maxton-Weir.'
Marty moves in dread towards the window – standing there
Draws the curtain – sees the guilty movement of the pair.[1]
White with rage and lined with age but strong and
      sturdy still
Marty now co-ordinates her passions and her will,
She will teach that Judy girl to trifle with the heart
And go and kiss a paratroop like any common tart.

---

[1] These lines in italic are by Henry Oscar.

She switches up the radiogram and covered by the
    blare
She goes and gets a riding whip and whirls it in the air,
She fetches down a length of rope and rushes, breathing
    hard
To let the couple have it for embracing in the yard.
Crack! the pair are paralysed. Click! they cannot stir.
Zip! she's trussed the paratroop. There's no embracing
    her.
'Hullo, hullo, hullo, hullo . . . Major Maxton-Weir?
I've trussed your missing paratroop. He's waiting for
    you here.'

Seaside Golf

How straight it flew, how long it flew,
    It clear'd the rutty track
And soaring, disappeared from view
    Beyond the bunker's back -
A glorious, sailing, bounding drive
That made me glad I was alive.

And down the fairway, far along
    It glowed a lonely white;
I played an iron sure and strong
    And clipp'd it out of sight,
And spite of grassy banks between
I knew I'd find it on the green.

And so I did. It lay content
    Two paces from the pin;
A steady putt and then it went
    Oh, most securely in.
The very turf rejoiced to see
That quite unprecedented three.

Ah! seaweed smells from sandy caves
    And thyme and mist in whiffs,
In-coming tide, Atlantic waves
    Slapping the sunny cliffs,
Lark song and sea sounds in the air
And splendour, splendour everywhere.

Sun and Fun

SONG OF A NIGHT CLUB PROPRIETRESS

I walked into the night club in the morning,
    There was kummel on the handle of the door,
The ashtrays were unemptied,
The cleaning unattempted,
    And a squashed tomato sandwich on the floor.

I pulled aside the thick magenta curtains
    – So Regency, so Regency, my dear –
And a host of little spiders
Ran a race across the ciders
    To a box of baby 'pollies by the beer.

Oh sun upon the summer-going by-pass
    Where ev'rything is speeding to the sea,
And wonder beyond wonder
That here where lorries thunder
    The sun should ever percolate to me.

When Boris used to call in his Sedanca,
    When Teddy took me down to his estate,
When my nose excited passion,
When my clothes were in the fashion,
    When my beaux were never cross if I was late,

There was sun enough for lazing upon beaches,
    There was fun enough for far into the night.
But I'm dying now and done for,
What on earth was all the fun for?
    For I'm old and ill and terrified and tight.

Hunter Trials

It's awf'lly bad luck on Diana,
    Her ponies have swallowed their bits;
She fished down their throats with a spanner
    And frightened them all into fits.

So now she's attempting to borrow.
    Do lend her some bits, Mummy, *do*;
I'll lend her my own for to-morrow,
    But to-day *I'll* be wanting them too.

Just look at Prunella on Guzzle,
    The wizardest pony on earth;
Why doesn't she slacken his muzzle
    And tighten the breech in his girth?

I say, Mummy, there's Mrs Geyser
    And doesn't she look pretty sick?
I bet it's because Mona Lisa
    Was hit on the hock with a brick.

Miss Blewitt says Monica threw it,
    But Monica says it was Joan,
And Joan's very thick with Miss Blewitt,
    So Monica's sulking alone.

And Margaret failed in her paces,
    Her withers got tied in a noose,
So her coronets caught in the traces
    And now all her fetlocks are loose.

Oh, it's me now. I'm terribly nervous.
  I wonder if Smudges will shy.
She's practically certain to swerve as
  Her Pelham is over one eye.

     ★   ★   ★   ★   ★

Oh wasn't it naughty of Smudges?
  Oh, Mummy, I'm sick with disgust.
She threw me in front of the Judges,
  And my silly old collarbone's bust.

JOHN BETJEMAN

False Security

I remember the dread with which I at a quarter past
    four
Let go with a bang behind me our house front door
And, clutching a present for my dear little hostess tight,
Sailed out for the children's party into the night
Or rather the gathering night. For still some boys
In the near municipal acres were making a noise
Shuffling in fallen leaves and shouting and whistling
And running past hedges of hawthorn, spikey and
    bristling.
And black in the oncoming darkness stood out the trees
And pink shone the ponds in the sunset ready to freeze
And all was still and ominous waiting for dark
And the keeper was ringing his closing bell in the park
And the arc lights started to fizzle and burst into mauve
As I climbed West Hill to the great big house in The
    Grove,
Where the children's party was and the dear little
    hostess.
But halfway up stood the empty house where the ghost
    is.
I crossed to the other side and under the arc
Made a rush for the next kind lamp-post out of the dark
And so to the next and the next till I reached the top
Where the Grove branched off to the left. Then ready to
    drop
I ran to the ironwork gateway of number seven
Secure at last on the lamplit fringe of Heaven.
Oh who can say how subtle and safe one feels
Shod in one's children's sandals from Daniel Neal's,
Clad in one's party clothes made of stuff from Heal's?
And who can still one's thrill at the candle shine

On cakes and ices and jelly and blackcurrant wine,
And the warm little feel of my hostess's hand in mine?
Can I forget my delight at the conjuring show?
And wasn't I proud that I was the last to go?
Too overexcited and pleased with myself to know
That the words I heard my hostess's mother employ
To a guest departing, would ever diminish my joy,
I WONDER WHERE JULIA FOUND THAT STRANGE, RATHER
    COMMON LITTLE BOY?

Executive

I am a young executive. No cuffs than mine are cleaner;
I have a Slimline brief-case and I use the firm's Cortina.
In every roadside hostelry from here to Burgess Hill
The *maîtres d'hôtel* all know me well and let me sign the
    bill.

You ask me what it is I do. Well actually, you know,
I'm partly a liaison man and partly PRO.
Essentially I integrate the current export drive
And basically I'm viable from ten o'clock till five.

For vital off-the-record work – that's talking
    transport-wise –
I've a scarlet Aston-Martin – and does she go? She flies!
Pedestrians and dogs and cats – we mark them down for
    slaughter.
I also own a speed-boat which has never touched the
    water.

She's built of fibre-glass, of course. I call her 'Mandy
    Jane'
After a bird I used to know – No soda, please, just plain
And how did I acquire her? Well to tell you about that
And to put you in the picture I must wear my other hat.

I do some mild developing. The sort of place I need
Is a quiet country market town that's rather run to
    seed.
A luncheon and a drink or two, a little *savoir faire* –
I fix the Planning Officer, the Town Clerk and the
    Mayor.

And if some preservationist attempts to interfere
A 'dangerous structure' notice from the Borough
    Engineer
Will settle any buildings that are standing in our way –
The modern style, sir, with respect, has really come to
    stay.

Notes

Trebetherick

Notice how the rhythm changes where the longer lines start.
First of all there's the slow, pacing part, and then it goes into a
lolloping, tub-thumping sort of gallop. It's not exactly like the
repeated refrain of a song – though the line with the names of
the children *is* repeated – but it works in much the same way.
What do you think about the grim section – the 'shade of evil'
and the rabbit and pheasant 'torn open at the throat'? Does it fit
in? What about your own recollections of the seaside? Try a
poem from your own childhood about making sandcastles,
going out in a rowing boat – or even about just *wanting* to do
these things. Work in some strange names that mean a lot to
you: names of friends and names of places (e.g. Dunoon,
Bridlington, Hastings, Blackpool, Lyme Regis, Rothesay). Then
list all the first names of the other people in your class – girls or
boys or both – and arrange them in the order that sounds best.
Try chanting them aloud all together; then one after the other –
like a roll call – but for music, not for sequence.

A Shropshire Lad

This should be spoken aloud – like a comedian's monologue –
with a Midlands accent. Everyone might come in on the chorus
at the end of each section – swimming along, etc. Captain Webb
– he used to be on the back of matchboxes – was the first man to
swim the channel. He was born in Dawley. *A Shropshire Lad* –

which Webb was – is the title of a famous book of poems by the late nineteenth-century poet A E Housman. It isn't often that you get a ghost story which is funny. Can you think of another one? You might like to dream up a ghost story of your own which isn't funny. See if you can locate it in a part of the country – your own street, if you like – that you know well. Give it body by using real names: Hangingwater Road, Clapham Common, Sauchiehall Street.

In Westminster Abbey

A satire on – or send-up of – a posh lady thinking she is so important that all her prayers – however vicious – will immediately be answered. It was written during the Second World War, but you could change the word 'Germans' to 'Russians' or 'Argies' or anything else you like, and it would still hold force. Go round the class, taking one section each, and try to imitate a pompous old woman praying.

On a Portrait of a Deaf Man

Another poem which addresses God, but this time a lot more seriously. Do you think enough is made of the man's deafness? Or is that only drawn attention to in order to make the title vivid? If so, is that fair? Notice how all five of the senses are worked into the poem – the mouth for potatoes, the nose for the smell of ploughed-up soil, the hands for handshaking, the eyes for, well, maggots and painting, and the ears for not hearing with. Notice how the tie is described as 'loud'. Imagine losing one of your own senses: touch, for example. Imagine doing everything in gloves – everything. Would your other senses grow sharper? Imagine being blind and trying to kiss somebody. What do you least like to eat? Would you mind if you couldn't taste it?

from *Summoned by Bells*

There can't be many English poems as exclusively nose-conscious as this. A dog would see the point. Have a go at a sound passage in the same style. Close your eyes and listen. Try to build up a picture in words based entirely on what you can hear. Yes, now, in the classroom. Do you hear giggling? Motorcars? Chalk on a blackboard? Your own clothes rustling?

Invasion Exercise on the Poultry Farm

This is a Second World War poem. 'Craven A' was a kind of cigarette. You might like to try doing the whole poem as a kind of play. Try and set the scene and replace the descriptive passages by mime or noises. (Telephone, owls, door slamming shouldn't be hard.) Plenty of scope for fun in the whipping bit at the end ...

Seaside Golf

An iron is a kind of golf club. You might like to try a passionate poem about, say, cricket or snooker or table tennis, in the same vein.

What joy to see the flying bails!
The flannels white as billowing sails ...

Sun and Fun

A poem spoken by an ageing 'madame'. Imagine a good character actress reading this poem. Or think of someone you know, who's a bit drunk, and sadly going over the past. (Kummel is a Dutch liqueur; a Sedanca was a kind of car.) You might like to try bringing the poem up to date, and down to your own – or your parents' – age level. Imagine waking up with a bad headache after a party or feeling you are old already – remembering Melville with his Harley Davidson motorbike.

Hunter Trials

Do you find this poem comic and silly? Or does it seem touching and tender? Or a bit of both? If you like the poem, and can ride, write a poem about a horse. If you don't like the poem, write about your motorbike or your disco skates. Work in some slang you use yourself or you hear friends using. Forget the rhyme and rhythm – just use absolutely natural phrases.

False Security

A poem set in Highgate, in North London. The match between the long, loose lines and the tight rhymes is an unusual one. It's an effect often used for humour by the American poet Ogden Nash, but here Betjeman is serious even – or perhaps particularly – with that last quote in small capital letters. Do you ever have to go for a walk in the dark that makes you frightened? Or did you, when you were younger? Try to recall your feelings. Mention buildings or parks or streets that you tried to avoid or go past quickly. Don't necessarily mention why, just make them sound frightening. Then try to work in something which somebody once said that you found very wounding and hurtful – for example, 'nigger', 'cissy', 'cleverdick', 'little bitch', or 'moron'. Don't say why, just quote it.

Executive

Maître d'hôtel is a kind of head waiter. PRO is a Public Relations Officer. There is scope here for some more sarcastic voicing. Practise a very false, pseudo-military sort of accent for this character. Who could he be? Edward Fox? Try to think of an actor you've seen on television who could do the executive well. If you know their faces but not their names, look them up in the *Radio Times* or *TV Times*.

Philip Larkin

Philip Larkin was born in Coventry, worked in Belfast for a time, and has for many years been the librarian at the University of Hull. He used to have a large desk in his office there, as large almost as the Italian dictator Mussolini's, with a photograph of Guy, the famous gorilla from London Zoo, at one end. This taste for a kind of flamboyant control, deflated by a self-mocking irony, is typical of Philip Larkin in his poetry. As one would expect from a man who spends his life with books, it's a poetry very much affected – and to its advantage – by what he's read. But a deep suspicion of 'bookishness', of the tendency to be too clever, has led him to go for a plain, even sometimes slangy and dirty-worded, style. Larkin's poems usually rhyme, and he's one of the best examples in this anthology of a poet who tries to make his verse sound like natural talk, even when the structure he's chosen may look like an old-fashioned three-piece suit. As well as poetry, Larkin has written jazz criticism, and, when younger, two novels, but his love affair with poetry – he thinks that poets shouldn't get married – has been a constant and long-lasting one, even though sparingly consummated: only three collections in thirty years. Can one write too little? Do you think that the high quality of Larkin's poetry depends on him having written so sparingly?

Money

Quarterly, is it, money reproaches me:
    'Why do you let me lie here wastefully?
I am all you never had of goods and sex.
    You could get them still by writing a few cheques.'

So I look at others, what they do with theirs:
    They certainly don't keep it upstairs.
By now they've a second house and car and wife:
    Clearly money has something to do with life

– In fact, they've a lot in common, if you enquire:
    You can't put off being young until you retire,
And however you bank your screw, the money you save
    Won't in the end buy you more than a shave.

I listen to money singing. It's like looking down
    From long french windows at a provincial town,
The slums, the canal, the churches ornate and mad
    In the evening sun. It is intensely sad.

Annus Mirabilis

Sexual intercourse began
In nineteen sixty-three
(Which was rather late for me) –
Between the end of the *Chatterley* ban
And the Beatles' first LP.

Up till then there'd only been
A sort of bargaining,
A wrangle for a ring,
A shame that started at sixteen
And spread to everything.

Then all at once the quarrel sank:
Everyone felt the same,
And every life became
A brilliant breaking of the bank,
A quite unlosable game.

So life was never better than
In nineteen sixty-three
(Though just too late for me) –
Between the end of the *Chatterley* ban
And the Beatles' first LP.

Homage to a Government

Next year we are to bring the soldiers home
For lack of money, and it is all right.
Places they guarded, or kept orderly,
Must guard themselves, and keep themselves orderly.
We want the money for ourselves at home
Instead of working. And this is all right.

It's hard to say who wanted it to happen,
But now it's been decided nobody minds.
The places are a long way off, not here,
Which is all right, and from what we hear
The soldiers there only made trouble happen.
Next year we shall be easier in our minds.

Next year we shall be living in a country
That brought its soldiers home for lack of money.
The statues will be standing in the same
Tree-muffled squares, and look nearly the same.
Our children will not know it's a different country.
All we can hope to leave them now is money.

1969

The Old Fools

What do they think has happened, the old fools,
To make them like this? Do they somehow suppose
It's more grown-up when your mouth hangs open and
        drools,
And you keep on pissing yourself, and can't remember
Who called this morning? Or that, if they only chose,
They could alter things back to when they danced all
        night,
Or went to their wedding, or sloped arms some
        September?
Or do they fancy there's really been no change,
And they've always behaved as if they were crippled or
        tight,
Or sat through days of thin continuous dreaming
Watching light move? If they don't (and they can't), it's
        strange:
                Why aren't they screaming?

At death, you break up: the bits that were you
Start speeding away from each other for ever
With no one to see. It's only oblivion, true:
We had it before, but then it was going to end,
And was all the time merging with a unique endeavour
To bring to bloom the million-petalled flower
Of being here. Next time you can't pretend
There'll be anything else. And these are the first signs:
Not knowing how, not hearing who, the power
Of choosing gone. Their looks show that they're for it:
Ash hair, toad hands, prune face dried into lines –
                How can they ignore it?

Perhaps being old is having lighted rooms
Inside your head, and people in them, acting.
People you know, yet can't quite name; each looms
Like a deep loss restored, from known doors turning,
Setting down a lamp, smiling from a stair, extracting
A known book from the shelves; or sometimes only
The rooms themselves, chairs and a fire burning,
The blown bush at the window, or the sun's
Faint friendliness on the wall some lonely
Rain-ceased midsummer evening. That is where they
    live:
Not here and now, but where all happened once.
       This is why they give

An air of baffled absence, trying to be there
Yet being here. For the rooms grow farther, leaving
Incompetent cold, the constant wear and tear
Of taken breath, and them crouching below
Extinction's alp, the old fools, never perceiving
How near it is. This must be what keeps them quiet:
The peak that stays in view wherever we go
For them is rising ground. Can they never tell
What is dragging them back, and how it will end? Not
    at night?
Not when the strangers come? Never, throughout
The whole hideous inverted childhood? Well,
      We shall find out.

Born Yesterday

for Sally Amis

Tightly-folded bud,
I have wished you something
None of the others would:
Not the usual stuff
About being beautiful,
Or running off a spring
Of innocence and love –
They will all wish you that,
And should it prove possible,
Well, you're a lucky girl.

But if it shouldn't, then
May you be ordinary;
Have, like other women,
An average of talents:
Not ugly, not good-looking,
Nothing uncustomary
To pull you off your balance,
That, unworkable itself,
Stops all the rest from working.
In fact, may you be dull –
If that is what a skilled,
Vigilant, flexible,
Unemphasised, enthralled
Catching of happiness is called.

I Remember, I Remember

Coming up England by a different line
For once, early in the cold new year,
We stopped, and, watching men with number-plates
Sprint down the platform to familiar gates,
'Why, Coventry!' I exclaimed. 'I was born here.'

I leant far out, and squinnied for a sign
That this was still the town that had been 'mine'
So long, but found I wasn't even clear
Which side was which. From where those cycle-crates
Were standing, had we annually departed

For all those family hols? . . . A whistle went:
Things moved. I sat back, staring at my boots.
'Was that,' my friend smiled, 'where you "have your
        roots"?'
No, only where my childhood was unspent,
I wanted to retort, just where I started:

By now I've got the whole place clearly charted.
Our garden, first: where I did not invent
Blinding theologies of flowers and fruits,
And wasn't spoken to by an old hat.
And here we have that splendid family

I never ran to when I got depressed,
The boys all biceps and the girls all chest,
Their comic Ford, their farm where I could be
'Really myself'. I'll show you, come to that,
The bracken where I never trembling sat,

Determined to go through with it; where she
Lay back, and 'all became a burning mist'.
And, in those offices, my doggerel
Was not set up in blunt ten-point, nor read
By a distinguished cousin of the mayor,

Who didn't call and tell my father *There
Before us, had we the gift to see ahead* –
'You look as if you wished the place in Hell,'
My friend said, 'judging from your face.' 'Oh well,
I suppose it's not the place's fault,' I said.

'Nothing, like something, happens anywhere.'

Reasons for Attendance

The trumpet's voice, loud and authoritative,
Draws me a moment to the lighted glass
To watch the dancers – all under twenty-five –
Shifting intently, face to flushed face,
Solemnly on the beat of happiness.

– Or so I fancy, sensing the smoke and sweat,
The wonderful feel of girls. Why be out here?
But then, why be in there? Sex, yes, but what
Is sex? Surely, to think the lion's share
Of happiness is found by couples – sheer

Inaccuracy, as far as I'm concerned.
What calls me is that lifted, rough-tongued bell
(Art, if you like) whose individual sound
Insists I too am individual.
It speaks; I hear; others may hear as well,

But not for me, nor I for them; and so
With happiness. Therefore I stay outside,
Believing this; and they maul to and fro,
Believing that; and both are satisfied,
If no one has misjudged himself. Or lied.

Notes

Money

It might be worth comparing this poem with Lawrence's *Money-Madness* (page 26). Which sounds the more natural to you? Lawrence's poem is in free verse, yes: but isn't Larkin more colloquial in his choice of words – 'screw', for instance? Then what about the feeling? Is Larkin too detached? Or is he just as downcast in his own mode as Lawrence is angry in his? Think about the way this poem is put together – the neatness of that rhyme of 'sex' with 'cheques'; the casual, sloping sort of rhythm where each idea or sentence seems to fill one line; and the rather grand, 'romantic' ending, like a fine Edwardian painting. What does the comparison of money 'singing' with the town mean? Is it meant to be crystal clear? Or is it perhaps meant to carry your mind out and away and make you think more widely and subtly? Try a poem yourself where you put down some simple, straightforward ideas – about school, perhaps, or old age – and then finish with some scene-painting comparison, like Larkin's. Going to school is like walking along a deserted seashore at mid-day, in a hailstorm. It can be so cold. That sort of thing, maybe.

Annus Mirabilis

The title means 'wonderful year' in Latin. *Chatterley* refers to D H Lawrence's famous novel *Lady Chatterley's Lover*, which was banned from publication for thirty years because it printed a four-letter word. It was in 1963, of course, that the Beatles first sprung to widespread fame. Larkin was forty-one that year. The poem works like a serious ballad, with a slightly varying refrain. It would be a nice exercise to try and set some music to it. You may find that the middle two stanzas have to be spoken, and the first and last one can be sung. Can you think of an 'annus mirabilis' of your own? It might be when your team won the championship, or when you got a school prize, or when you went somewhere special on holiday. Try to link up a public and a private event of importance: for example, the marriage of Prince Charles and Lady Diana and your first flight in an aeroplane. Make your own serious song about it.

Homage to a Government

This again is a downcast, rather than an angry, poem. But there's anger underneath, I think. In a world ruled by the laws of economics, the emphasis on money is natural. But it may not be the poet's own voice which is uppermost in the poem. The lines murmur along like the busy, repetitive hum of a large crowd, always going over and over the same handful of points. Larkin draws attention to this by his boring repetition of the same words at the ends of lines: home, home; orderly, orderly; right, right – and so on. He may be the mute witness to this awful acceptance, too paralyzed to say or do anything, except to poke fun at the irony of a once great imperial power in decline. Is he being a bit of an old reactionary here? Is that easy to be, emotionally, for someone born before the Second World War, do you think? Try dividing up the lines of the poem in class and murmuring them one after another, or even like a round, overlapping, one whole group starting to read later than another, until you get a big, vague hum of sound; then let individual voices murmur out and the whole thing die away. You might be able to orchestrate an interesting choral effect.

The Old Fools

This is Larkin in his more violent, frightened, disgusted, questioning mood. There's nothing here about old people being more wise, or more dignified, or more worthy of reverence than the young. Once again, it might be interesting to compare D H Lawrence with Larkin. In *The Grudge of the Old*, the mood is much the same as in *The Old Fools*, but for different reasons. Which poem is the more personal: Larkin's, perhaps? Do you think he might have in mind some particular old person – a parent or a friend – whom he feels deeply disturbed about? If so, why doesn't he say so? Is his poem all the stronger for not being reduced to one example? Or does it lose focus? Try a poem about someone old you know – a grandparent, maybe, or an old aunt or uncle. See if you can combine your own views about old age with some exact description. First think how good Larkin is using only six words of verbal sculpture: 'Ash hair, toad hands, prune face...'. That is what you have to beat.

Born Yesterday

This is a sort of birthday greeting card. It must have been nice to grow up with such a well-known poem to justify your not being very much. But notice how skilfully Larkin – like a good barrister – can redefine the unflattering word 'dull' and make it sound like high praise. Think of other ordinary words, without much glamour to them, and try to upgrade their significance by a string of four or five high-sounding equivalents. See what you can do with 'charm' or 'tact', for example. Try to make them sound the most remarkable qualities that ever were.

I Remember, I Remember

Start by working out how the rhyme-scheme in this poem goes on from stanza (or section) to stanza. It's clever and exact. Yes, but does 'mist' rhyme with 'chest'? Even Larkin may nod. Or is it one deliberate 'off' rhyme in a poem of precise rhymes? Which do you think? The argument works by negatives, everything mentioned is what the poet *didn't* do in his home town – as opposed, of course, to what other, more privileged, or more pretentious, autobiographers have claimed they did. In fact, it's a fairly baleful indictment of life in the Midlands, extended – if that's any excuse – only by the sonorous gloom of the last line. What is your own view of the place where you were born? Do you recall it, after moving, with regret or with hatred? Let's have a poem called: *My Cardiff*, or *My Glasgow*, or *Brixton: the way I see it*. Let your own emotions come out, rejecting the place, or glamorizing its attractions.

Reasons for Attendance

Notice here how the rhymes are 'off – as in off-key, if you like the effect, or milk that's gone off, perhaps, if you don't – until they grow strict in the last stanza. 'Glass' and 'face' will do, to begin with, but by the end it's as tight as 'lied' and 'satisfied'. This is obviously deliberate. But why? Well, perhaps the tone of the poem gets more high-flown as it progresses. Do you think it does? The message is something about the generation gap, feeling too old – as in *Annus Mirabilis* – to have fun. Yes, but it's also something about being willing to be alone and get something done. Then the wry comment in the last two words of the poem hints how people often disguise their true interests – as in sex questionnaires – and pretend they like something they don't. What about writing your own dance hall poem? Call it simply *Disco*, and try to get in what you feel when you're moving on a dance floor. Mention particular songs and bands, what it smells like, the effect on you of strobe lights, what a boy's – or a girl's – body feels like in your arms. Then imagine your father looking in through the window, and what he might think.

Ted Hughes

Ted Hughes was born in a small town in West Yorkshire. He went to school there, and then on to Cambridge, where he read English. For many years he has farmed in Devon, and his experience of the countryside – both in the North and the South – has given his poetry deep roots in the soil. Even when writing about an urban situation, or a machine, he can give his work the feel of Nature 'red in tooth and claw'. The vulnerable or sometimes threatening energy of animals is often the theme of Hughes's work, and no one has beaten him in emphasizing the heroic, and admirable, aspects of the natural world. Unlike earlier Nature poets – and a Romantic poet like Wordsworth comes to mind here – Hughes has failed to find a calm retreat, or a solace for metropolitan ills, or a lost Eden, in Nature. Instead, he grapples with the violence of the twentieth century, and the hatreds and tensions in the human psyche, by a profound grasp of what makes Nature tick: the basic need to flee or kill to survive.

The Bull Moses

A hoist up and I could lean over
The upper edge of the high half-door,
My left foot ledged on the hinge, and look in at the
    byre's
Blaze of darkness: a sudden shut-eyed look
Backward into the head.
                      Blackness is depth
Beyond star. But the warm weight of his breathing,
The ammoniac reek of his litter, the hotly-tongued
Mash of his cud, steamed against me.
Then, slowly, as onto the mind's eye –
The brow like masonry, the deep-keeled neck:
Something come up there onto the brink of the gulf,
Hadn't heard of the world, too deep in itself to be called
    to,
Stood in sleep. He would swing his muzzle at a fly
But the square of sky where I hung, shouting waving,
Was nothing to him; nothing of our light
Found any reflection in him.
                    Each dusk the farmer led him
Down to the pond to drink and smell the air,
And he took no pace but the farmer
Led him to take it, as if he knew nothing
Of the ages and continents of his fathers,
Shut, while he wombed, to a dark shed
And steps between his door and the duckpond;
The weight of the sun and the moon and the world
    hammered
To a ring of brass through his nostrils.
                        He would raise
His streaming muzzle and look out over the meadows,

But the grasses whispered nothing awake, the fetch
Of the distance drew nothing to momentum
In the locked black of his powers. He came strolling
    gently back,
Paused neither toward the pig-pens on his right,
Nor toward the cow-byres on his left: something
Deliberate in his leisure, some beheld future
Founding in his quiet.
                  I kept the door wide,
Closed it after him and pushed the bolt.

A March Calf

Right from the start he is dressed in his best – his blacks
    and his whites.
Little Fauntleroy – quiffed and glossy,
A Sunday suit, a wedding natty get-up,
Standing in dunged straw

Under cobwebby beams, near the mud wall,
Half of him legs,
Shining-eyed, requiring nothing more
But that mother's milk come back often.

Everything else is in order, just as it is.
Let the summer skies hold off, for the moment.
This is just as he wants it.
A little at a time, of each new thing, is best.

Too much and too sudden is too frightening –
When I block the light, a bulk from space,
To let him in to his mother for a suck,
He bolts a yard or two, then freezes,

Staring from every hair in all directions,
Ready for the worst, shut up in his hopeful religion,
A little syllogism
With a wet blue-reddish muzzle, for God's thumb.

You see all his hopes bustling
As he reaches between the worn rails towards
The topheavy oven of his mother.
He trembles to grow, stretching his curl-tip tongue –

What did cattle ever find here
To make this dear little fellow
So eager to prepare himself?
He is already in the race, and quivering to win –

His new purpled eyeball swivel-jerks
In the elbowing push of his plans.
Hungry people are getting hungrier,
Butchers developing expertise and markets,

But he just wobbles his tail – and glistens
Within his dapper profile
Unaware of how his whole lineage
Has been tied up.

He shivers for feel of the world licking his side.
He is like an ember – one glow
Of lighting himself up
With the fuel of himself, breathing and brightening.

Soon he'll plunge out, to scatter his seething joy,
To be present at the grass,
To be free on the surface of such a wideness,
To find himself himself. To stand. To moo.

The Stag

While the rain fell on the November woodland shoulder
of Exmoor
While the traffic jam along the road honked and
shouted
Because the farmers were parking wherever they could
And scrambling to the bank-top to stare through the
tree-fringe
Which was leafless,
The stag ran through his private forest.

While the rain drummed on the roofs of the parked cars
And the kids inside cried and daubed their chocolate
and fought
And mothers and aunts and grandmothers
Were a tangle of undoing sandwiches and
screwed-round gossiping heads
Steaming up the windows,
The stag loped through his favourite valley.

While the blue horsemen down in the boggy meadow
Sodden nearly black, on sodden horses,
Spaced as at a military parade,
Moved a few paces to the right and a few to the left and
felt rather foolish
Looking at the brown impassable river,
The stag came over the last hill of Exmoor.

While everybody high-kneed it to the bank-top all along
the road
Where steady men in oilskins were stationed at
binoculars,

And the horsemen by the river galloped anxiously this
      way and that
And the cry of hounds came tumbling invisibly with
      their echoes down through the draggle of trees,
Swinging across the wall of dark woodland,
The stag dropped into a strange country.

And turned at the river
Hearing the hound-pack smash the undergrowth,
      hearing the bell-note
Of the voice that carried all the others,
Then while his limbs all cried different directions to his
      lungs, which only wanted to rest,
The blue horsemen on the bank opposite
Pulled aside the camouflage of their terrible planet.

And the stag doubled back weeping and looking for
      home up a valley and down a valley
While the strange trees struck at him and the brambles
      lashed him,
And the strange earth came galloping after him
      carrying the loll-tongued hounds to fling all over
      him
And his heart became just a club beating his ribs and
      his own hooves shouted with hounds' voices,
And the crowd on the road got back into their cars
Wet-through and disappointed.

A Motorbike

We had a motorbike all through the war
In an outhouse – thunder, flight, disruption
Cramped in rust, under washing, abashed, outclassed
By the Brens, the Bombs, the Bazookas elsewhere.

The war ended, the explosions stopped.
The men surrendered their weapons
And hung around limply.
Peace took them all prisoner.
They were herded into their home towns.
A horrible privation began
Of working a life up out of the avenues
And the holiday resorts and the dance-halls.

Then the morning bus was as bad as any labour truck,
The foreman, the boss, as bad as the SS.
And the ends of the street and the bends of the road
And the shallowness of the shops and the shallowness of
     the beer
And the sameness of the next town
Were as bad as electrified barbed wire.
The shrunk-back war ached in their testicles
And England dwindled to the size of a dog-track.

So there came this quiet young man
And he bought our motorbike for twelve pounds.
And he got it going, with difficulty.
He kicked it into life – it erupted
Out of the six year sleep, and he was delighted.

A week later, astride it, before dawn,
A misty frosty morning,
He escaped

Into a telegraph pole
On the long straight west of Swinton.

Beware of the Stars

That star
Will blow your hand off

That star
Will scramble your brains and your nerves

That star
Will frizzle your skin off

That star
Will turn everybody yellow and stinking

That star
Will scorch everything dead fumed to its blueprint

That star
Will make the earth melt

That star . . . and so on.

And they surround us. And far into infinity.
These are the armies of the night.
We are totally surrounded.
There is no escape.
Not one of them is good, or friendly, or corruptible.

One chance remains: KEEP ON DIGGING THAT HOLE

KEEP ON DIGGING AWAY AT THAT HOLE

121

Notes

The Bull Moses

A child's eye view of something colossal: the huge, self-involved
bulk of the bull. Notice two things about the poem: the boy's
subdued sense of wonder at the power and dignity of the great
animal, and the grown poet's ability to recreate the childhood
experience in a vivid stew of smell images – 'the ammoniac reek
of his litter, the hotly-tongued mash of his cud'. Try to write
down the remembered stink of a farmyard for yourself – or
perhaps a butcher's or a fishmonger's shop. Close your eyes and
go for what you can take in through your nose. Have a look, too,
at the nose passage from John Betjeman's *Summoned by Bells*
(page 81).

A March Calf

This is the bull's offspring. A tender evocation of the first few
hours of life for a new being in a puzzling and perhaps
dangerous world. Imagine a poem about a human baby in the
same style. Could you get the same solidness in language –
'topheavy oven of his mother', 'wet blue-reddish muzzle' – in
describing a baby boy or girl? Think of a little brother or sister.
Then try a poem about the child Jesus, born in a stable,
surrounded by farm animals. Think of pictures in an old Bible
and use the Hughes style to bring them to life.

The Stag

You may have seen a painting of a stag, or a set of antlers on a
wall. Have you seen the real thing outside a zoo? Few people
have, largely because of hunting. This poem conveys the

122

excitement and vicarious, rather gloating fascination some people feel at the idea of a stag-hunt. But it may be a sort of moral emblem rather than a true picture. Do stags weep, for instance? No? Then what about willows? How far is the poet making you feel that *you* are the stag? Why not try a poem in the first person – using the word 'I' – where you aim to run yourself in front of the dogs? Become a hare, if you like, or a mouse being hunted by a cat.

A Motorbike

Motorbikes are often a symbol for getting away from it all. In this poem, the motorbike is a symbol for getting away from dullness; but getting away into death. Some of your fathers and mothers will remember the sense of boredom when the 1939–45 war ended. The widespread looking around for some new excitement to compensate for the loss of the blitz. Does that attitude seem unreal to you? Or is it only natural? Write something about the 'quiet young man' in this poem. Create a background history for him. Was he an ex-soldier who just missed seeing action? Did he have an urge towards suicide? Bring him up to date as a Hell's Angel and put him in leathers. Have you seen him in your town? Would you like to ride with him? Or do you disapprove of his need for speed?

Beware of the Stars

What's this poem about? Nuclear warfare – or some other, less explicit threat? Is the hole being dug for a fall-out shelter? Why not try and continue the star list? See if you can get another three really good ones. That star/ will burn a hole in your palm ... and so on. Make one or two of them funny or grotesque. That star/ will turn into a Martian and fill itself up at the nearest petrol pump. Anything goes. Be as wild or nonsensical as you like.

Kit Wright

Kit Wright was born in Kent, towards the end of the Second World War. He has worked as a school teacher in a London comprehensive and as a lecturer in a Canadian university. As a reader of his own poems he has travelled widely, both in this country and in the United States, and he has written songs – which he puts over himself – and verse for small children as well as poetry. Kit Wright is one of the tightest poets in this book, and at the same time is one of the most free and direct in theme. Indeed, there are several excellent poems of his – notably a send-up of the radio show *The Archers* – which are too shocking to be included in an anthology likely to fall into the hands of unprotected teachers. A comparison between Kit Wright and Brian Patten – and there are only two year's age difference between them – will show how two largely urban poets of the same generation can adopt very differing technical means to get their message across. Verse can be either strict or free, in either case. There is more than one way to kill a cat.

Every Day in Every Way

(DR COUE: EVERY DAY IN EVERY WAY I GROW BETTER AND BETTER)

When I got up this morning
I thought the whole thing through:
Thought, Who's the hero, the man of the day?
Christopher, it's you.

With my left arm I raised my right arm
High above my head:
Said, Christopher, you're the greatest.
Then I went back to bed.

I wrapped my arms around me,
No use counting sheep.
I counted legions of myself
Walking on the deep.

The sun blazed on the miracle,
The blue ocean smiled:
We like the way you operate,
Frankly, we like your style.

Dreamed I was in a meadow,
Angels singing hymns,
Fighting the nymphs and shepherds
Off my holy limbs.

A girl leaned out with an apple,
Said, You can taste for free.
I never touch the stuff, dear,
I'm keeping myself for me.

Dreamed I was in heaven,
God said, Over to you,
Christopher, you're the greatest!
And Oh, it's true, it's true!

I like my face in the mirror,
I like my voice when I sing.
My girl says it's just infatuation –
I know it's the real thing.

Red Boots On

Way down Geneva,
All along Vine,
Deeper than the snow drift
Love's eyes shine:

Mary Lou's walking
In the winter time.

She's got

Red boots on, she's got
Red boots on,
Kicking up the winter
Till the winter's gone.

So

Go by Ontario,
Look down Main,
If you can't find Mary Lou,
Come back again:

Sweet light burning
In winter's flame.

She's got

Snow in her eyes, got
A tingle in her toes
And new red boots on
Wherever she goes

So

All around Lake Street,
Up by St Paul,
Quicker than the white wind
Love takes all:

Mary Lou's walking
In the big snow fall.

She's got

Red boots on, she's got
Red boots on,
Kicking up the winter
Till the winter's gone.

A Doll's House

A man sat staring at a doll's house
Hour after hour and more and more
He believed. He could see
In the kitchenette two personettes
And one of them was standing in the sink
And one lay on the floor.

The man stared more and more.

The bed in the bathroom was neatly made up with a
Pink eiderdown neatly made up from a
Pink ribbon. But no-one was in the bed
And no-one was in the bathroom.
Only a horse
Was trying the door.

The man stared more and more.

Then softly the man went in,
Edged down
Past the creaky banisters, down
He crept
To the hall, hid nimbly
Behind a cow.

From the sink: 'My dear,
That tractor's on the roof again, I fear.'
Sadly from the floor: 'These nights
It seems to be always there.'

Then silence between
Personette A and Personette B,
Now like a matchstick drumming a plastic thimble,
Now like the sea.

From the sink: 'How I wish, my dear,
That you and I could move house.
But these matters are not in our hands. Our directives
Come from above.'
Said the floor: 'How can we ever move house
When the house keeps moving, my love?'

A man sat staring at a doll's house
Hour after hour and more and more
He believed he could see
Perspectives of the terrorized world,
Delicate, as a new-tooled body,
Monstrous, mad as he.

The Dark Night of the Sole

'My husband's an odd fish,' she said.
    A casual remark
And yet it lingered in my head
And later, when we went to bed,
    It woke me in the dark.

My husband's an odd fish. I lay
    Uneasy. On the ceiling
Raw lorry-lights strobe-lit the grey
Glimmer of dawn. Sleepless dismay
    Revolved upon the feeling

Of something wrong in what I'd heard,
    Some deep, unhappy thing,
Some *odder* fact her statement blurred.
And then a prickling horror stirred
    Within me as the wing

Of madness brushed. I recognized
    The real thing strange to be
Not dorsal structure (fins disguised)
Nor travel habits (route revised:
    A Day Return to sea)

But that he was a fish at all!
    Trembling, I left the bed,
Dressed quickly, tiptoed through the hall,
Edged past him, gaping from his stall
    Of oval water, fled

To where I sit and write these lines,
  Sweating. I saw and heard
Strange things last night. Cold guilt defines
The moral: learn to read the signs –
  She was an odd, odd bird.

Elizabeth

(In the summer of 1968 thousands of people turned out at the small stations along the route to see the train carrying the body of Robert Kennedy from New York to Arlington Memorial Cemetery in Washington. In Elizabeth, New Jersey, three people were pressed forward on to the line by the crowd and killed by a train coming the other way – I happened to be travelling up by the next train in this direction and passed the bodies. One was of a black woman.)

Up from Philadelphia,
Kennedy on my mind,
Found you waiting in Elizabeth,
Lying there by the line.

Up from Philadelphia,
Wasn't going back,
Saw you, then saw your handbag
Forty yards on up the track.

Saw you under a blanket,
Black legs sticking through,
Thought a lot about Kennedy,
Thought a lot about you.

Years later,

Blood on the line, blood on the line,
Elizabeth,
No end, no end to anything,
Nor any end to death.

No public grief by television,
Weeping all over town,
Nobody locked the train up
That struck the mourners down.

Nobody came to see you,
You weren't lying in state.
They swept you into a siding
And said the trains would be late.

They left you there in the siding
Against an outhouse wall
And the democratic primaries,
Oh they weren't affected at all,

In no way,

Blood on the line, blood on the line,
Elizabeth,
No end, no end to anything,
Nor any end to death.

Sirhan shot down Kennedy,
A bullet in L.A.,
But the one that broke Elizabeth,
It was coming the other way,

Coming on out of nowhere,
Into nowhere sped,
Blind as time, my darling,
Blind nothing in its head.

Elizabeth, Oh Elizabeth,
I cry your name and place
But you can't see under a blanket,
You can't see anyone's face,

Crying

Blood on the line, blood on the line,
Elizabeth,
No end, no end to anything,
Nor any end to death.

The Other Side of the Mountain

The bear barged into the boozer
To see what he could see.
And what do you think he saw
Behind the boozer door?

The other bar of the boozer
On the other side of the boozer,
The other side of the boozer
On the other side of the bar.

Which he had seen before.

So

The bear barged out of the boozer,
He didn't get too far.
And what do you think he saw
Outside the boozer door?

The door of another boozer
Outside the door of the boozer,
Outside the door of the boozer
A boozer door ajar.

So

The bear barged into the boozer
To see what he could see
And what do you think he saw
Behind the boozer door?

Another bear in the boozer,
The bar of the other boozer,
Another bear in the boozer
Whom he had seen before.

For

The other bear in the boozer,
The bear in the other boozer,
(The boozer outside the boozer)
Was not another boozer
But a bear inside the bear.

Cold Up Here

Oh

There's humour in height
And daily dully
In bar and café
And queue and crowd

They climb the long
Joke of my length.
Is it cold up there
Never mind you'll grow

Here lighthouse you give me a crick in the neck
I'll bet it's tricky
On the job though
Son.

Seldom offended,
Normally bored,
I was only once amused. In Perth
Two drunks singing YOU MUST HAVE BEEN A
    BLOODY GREAT BABY.

And I suppose
I must have been.
And sitting sprawled
In a waste of legs,

Hovering crane-like
Over conversations,
Confronting my geography
In a full-length mirror –

Feet at Lands End,
Whales of eyes
Mooning marooned
By Greenland –

It occurs to me: still am.
I see how the very tall
Are equated with a special kind
Of idiocy, the awkward vehicles

Of inanity
And cosmic uselessness.
Seldom offended,
Normally bored

And actually twice amused –
Motionless in a cinema queue –
IF YOU'RE GOING TO STAND THERE FOR
    CHRISTSAKE OPEN YOUR LEGS –
I am compelled to wonder

What is it lopes and blunders
With me through my life.
For it does get cold up here.
When I get drunk

I sway like a larch.
Hungover, a great condemned elm.
Sober me
Gangles and dangles.

And it does get cold up here. So here's
A message to all similar streaks of piss,
All hicks and loners,
Megagnomes and monopoles

And all the sundry other
Human hovercraft:
LET US NOT LOOM, my friends.
Let us make a vocation of tallness,

Go strutting under the moon,
Policemen edging under our crotches,
Straddle town halls and buffet the sun.
Let us walk in superior elements,

Knees nuzzling the lips of girls
(For we shall be gracious)
And there shall be no boredom
Stalking through the stars.

Notes

Every Day in Every Way

A good poem for when you're feeling down in the mouth. In the fourth section, remember it was Jesus Christ – half of Christopher, after all – who performed the miracle of walking on the water. It was the serpent, Satan, who offered Eve the apple – fruit of the tree of Knowledge – in the garden of Eden. So 'taste for free' might mean have me without sin. All this goes to show that it's quite a religious – or blasphemous? – poem under the jaunty surface. Does this worry you? Does it bore you? Write your own poem about a passing mood in which you see yourself as someone in the Bible.

It was so wet this morning, me and my dog felt like Noah. David, I said to myself, you'll feel better if you go out and find yourself a Goliath . . . and so on.

Red Boots On

One of the purest song-poems in this book. Why do you think that is? Perhaps you don't think it is? Does the American setting help? Are we too quick to connect American-sounding references with an American tone of voice, and thus the American accent of the rock singer? Anyway, is it America? Might it not be Canada? You might like to try a musical setting for Kit Wright's poem. See how it sounds. Imagine a painting of Mary Lou – an L S Lowry style painting, maybe – in a wintry landscape, red boots on total white. How much of the poem would you have to leave out of the painting? What could the painting usefully add? Would it help to show the colour of her eyes?

A Doll's House

Notice how the occasional rhymes are slotted in. Remember that everything doesn't need to rhyme in a poem – one or two rhymes may help. The Norwegian playwright, Ibsen, wrote a play called *The Doll's House*. Kit Wright may have the enclosed Scandinavian violence of someone like Ibsen in mind. On the other hand, it may be a fantasy based on staring down into a doll's house, and wondering what life in there must be like. What about the last three lines of the poem, though? What do they mean? Are they necessary? Imagine a different ending for this poem – and write it in Kit Wright's style – where the situation develops further, without the last three lines. The man turns round, perhaps, and his wife tells him to go out and lock up the horse. Or he shrinks in size and one of the personettes says to the other: 'Look, we've got a burglar.' ... or, 'Hello, God'.

The Dark Night of the Sole

Sole, soul: of course. A sort of comic – or perhaps not quite so comic – horror poem. Try writing the sequel – about a man married to an odd bird (include feathers, eggs, laying). Do it in prose, first; then try and line it up, and slot in some rhymes. Do you know the stories of Stephen King? You might get some horror tips from him, or some other contemporary horror writer. If you're short of ideas, go to a bookstall – after school – and glance along the rack of books with frightening covers.

Elizabeth

Do you think this is in any way a political poem? Or is it a poem about the general tragedy of people dying and being killed?

143

What about the song-like repetitions? Do you think they help the intensity of the poem, to bring across the poet's feeling more? Have you ever been in a big crowd – at a football match, say, or to watch a procession – and seen someone on the ground under a blanket, having fainted, or having a fit, or having been hit by something? Try and recall that moment and your feelings – or invent such a moment, if you can't remember one – and write what you remember or invent as a song.

The Other Side of the Mountain

Try your own play on words, expanding the kind of verbal trickery that Kit Wright uses here. Start with his own words. Try changing the vowels: burr, beer, byre, bore, boar, bare; buzzer, baize, er, abuser, abaser, and so on. See if you can weave some of those into a story with music. How about a bore who's always pressing a buzzer? Then try your wits on Kit Wright's own name: cut, cute, Kate, parakeet, coat, kite; rot, root, wrought, rut, wrote. Then see if you can combine these into some sort of celebratory – or, if you like, condemnatory – verses.

Kit Wright was not in a rut.

It was cute what he wrote ... or something.

Cold Up Here

Kit Wright himself is very tall, about six foot seven (2m). Imagine a similar poem about being fat, or short. We all have our own cross to bear. Pick on yours, and make it into a humorous poem. Work in all the jokes – cruel or good natured – and triumph over them. Add some boasts of your own.

I'm so fat my friends never need to buy a football.

But never mind.

We fat people can bounce our own way to beauty ... and so on.

Brian Patten

Brian Patten was born in Liverpool, and first came to the fore in the late 1960s, at a time when Liverpool was famous as the home of the Beatles, and the cradle of British pop music. The links between the so-called 'Liverpool poets' and the pop bands were close. For example, Paul McCartney's brother, Mike McGear, worked with Patten's friend and fellow poet, Roger McGough, in the chart-topping group, The Scaffold. Some people have suggested that Patten talks with the accent and the wit that the Beatles used in confronting the Press. But his tone of voice is richer, and less throwaway, than this. The effect of his best poems – particularly when spoken aloud in his own dwelling intonation – has more of the depth and swell of a good song by Bob Dylan. The rough humour, and the intense feeling, is often in the ideas, the music is in the interlacing of the words, and it stays strong and clear on the page.

A Blade of Grass

You ask for a poem.
I offer you a blade of grass.
You say it is not good enough.
You ask for a poem.

I say this blade of grass will do.
It has dressed itself in frost,
It is more immediate
Than any image of my making.

You say it is not a poem,
It is a blade of grass and grass
Is not quite good enough.
I offer you a blade of grass.

You are indignant.
You say it is too easy to offer grass.
It is absurd.
Anyone can offer a blade of grass.

You ask for a poem.
And so I write you a tragedy about
How a blade of grass
Becomes more and more difficult to offer,

And about how as you grow older
A blade of grass
Becomes more difficult to accept.

Somewhere between Heaven and Woolworth's
A Song

She keeps kingfishers in their cages
And goldfish in their bowls,
She is lovely and is afraid
Of such things as growing cold.

She's had enough men to please her
Though they were more cruel than kind
And their love an act in isolation,
A form of pantomime.

She says she has forgotten
The feelings that she shared
At various all-night parties
Among the couples on the stairs,

For among the songs and dancing
She was once open wide,
A girl dressed in denim
With boys dressed in lies.

She's eating roses on toast with tulip butter,
Praying for her mirror to stay young;
On its no longer gilted surface
This message she has scrawled:

'O somewhere between Heaven and Woolworth's
I live I love I scold,
I keep kingfishers in their cages
And goldfish in their bowls.'

Sometimes It Happens

And sometimes it happens that you are friends and then
You are not friends,
And friendship has passed.
And whole days are lost and among them
A fountain empties itself.

And sometimes it happens that you are loved and then
You are not loved,
And love is past.
And whole days are lost and among them
A fountain empties itself into the grass.

And sometimes you want to speak to her and then
You do not want to speak,
Then the opportunity has passed.
Your dreams flare up, they suddenly vanish.

And also it happens that there is nowhere to go and
    then
There is somewhere to go,
Then you have bypassed.
And the years flare up and are gone,
Quicker than a minute.

So you have nothing.
You wonder if these things matter and then
They cease to matter,
And caring is past.
And a fountain empties itself into the grass.

The Wrong Number

One night I went through the telephone book name by
    name.
    I moved in alphabetical order through London
Plundering living-rooms, basements, attics,
    Brothels and embassies.
I phoned florists' shops and mortuaries,
    Politicians and criminals with a flair for crime;
At midnight I phoned butchers and haunted them with
        strange bleatings,
    I phoned prisons and zoos simultaneously,
I phoned eminent surgeons at exactly the wrong
        moment.
    Before I was half-way through the phone book
My finger was numb and bloody.
    Not satisfied with the answers I tried again.
Moving frantically from A to Z needing confirmation
    That I was not alone.
I phoned grand arsonists who lived in the suburbs
    And rode bicycles made out of flames.
No doubt my calls disturbed people on their deathbeds,
    Their death rattles drowned by the constant ringing
        of telephones!
No doubt the various angels who stood beside them
    Thought me a complete nuisance.
I *was* a complete nuisance.
    I worried jealous husbands to distraction
And put various Casanovas off their stroke
    And woke couples drugged on love.
I kept the entire London telephone system busy,
    Darting from phone booth to phone booth
The Metropolitan phone-squad always one call behind
    me.

I sallied forth dressed in loneliness and paranoia –
The Phantom Connection.
Moving from shadow to shadow,
Rushing from phone booth to phone booth till finally
I sought out a forgotten number and dialled it.
A voice crackling with despair answered.
I recognised my own voice and had nothing to say to it.

Conversation with a Favourite Enemy

At a dinner party in aid of some unsufferable event
I sit opposite my favourite enemy.
'How's the cabbage?' he smiles.
'Fine,' I say, 'How's your novels?'
Something nasty has started.
On the chicken casserole the hairs bristle.
On the hostess the hairs bristle.
She glances down the dinner table
her eyes eloquent as politicians.
'Do you find the dumplings to your liking?' she asks,
'Do you find them juicy?'
'Fine,' I say, 'How's your daughter?'
She chokes on the melon.
After supper he's back again,
Wits sharpened on the brandy.
He folds his napkin into the shape of a bird,
'Can you make this sing?' he gloats,
'Would you say it's exactly poetry?'
Ah, but I'm lucky this evening!
In a tree outside a nightingale bursts into fragments.
It flings a shrapnel of song against the window.
My enemy ducks, but far too slowly.
It is not always like this.
My enemies are more articulate,
The nightingale, utterly unreliable.

Waves

And the one throwing the lifebelt,
Even he needs help at times,
Stranded on the beach,
Terrified of the waves.

Little Johnny's Confession

This morning
   being rather young and foolish
   I borrowed a machinegun my father
   had left hidden since the war, went out,
   and eliminated a number of small enemies.
   Since then I have not returned home.

This morning
   swarms of police with trackerdogs
   wander about the city
   with my description printed
   on their minds, asking:
   'Have you seen him?
   He is seven years old,
   likes Pluto, Mighty Mouse
   and Biffo the Bear,
   have you seen him, anywhere?'

This morning
   sitting alone in a strange playground
   muttering you've blundered, you've blundered
   over and over to myself
   I work out my next move
   but cannot move.
   The trackerdogs will sniff me out,
   they have my lollypops.

Notes

A Blade of Grass

This is a poem about simplicity, and about accepting the world as it is, unadorned, and with a child-like innocence. Well, yes, but it's also a poem about accepting a blade of grass. Patten's poems are often themselves, just as they are, and don't profit from being broken up and analysed. Is it true, though, that a blade of grass becomes harder to accept as you grow older? Think about Lawrence again, *The Grudge of the Old* (page 28), and Larkin's *The Old Fools* (page 101). Which is the saddest poem? Isn't there something tragic – about the fear of ageing perhaps – about Patten's poem? Think of some other simple things that might be offered: a glass of water, an autumn leaf, a grey hair. How might a poem about one of those develop?

Somewhere Between Heaven and Woolworth's

Notice the roughness of the rhyming in this poem. Sometimes it's no more than a common vowel, like 'bowls' and 'cold', sometimes it isn't there at all. The loose pattern of there *being* some rhyme helps to give the poem a kind of formality. Notice how the ending – as in Larkin's *Annus Mirabilis* – repeats the beginning. Try to make a song out of the poem. You may find here that the whole poem sings more easily than Larkin's. Why? Is it because Patten has a song writer like John Lennon or Bob Dylan in mind? Or because the mood is more song-like?

Sometimes it Happens

Notice how often sentences begin with 'and' in this poem. Do you think this adds to the rather biblical feel of the language? Do you know the Book of Ecclesiastes in the Bible? Look up Chapter XII and read the first seven verses. Isn't there something similar in Patten's poem: the mysteriousness of the fountain, the way phrases are repeated, and some balanced against each other, the mood of resignation? Is the feeling stronger for the use of this 'high' style? Try writing a poem about the death of somebody close to you – it could either be real or imaginary, but try to *feel* it as real – and use a solemn, biblical style.

The Wrong Number

This one works like a short story with a sting in the tail. You suddenly find the laugh wiped off your face. But it *is* funny, too, and it's the mixture of zany comedy and grim seriousness that finally makes it so good. Do you feel the rhythm is too near to prose? Try writing a similar piece – but not in verse – about, say, writing letters to all sorts of odd people, all over England, ending up, perhaps, with getting one back, and opening it, and finding it written by yourself. Then tighten it up by arranging it in longish lines, as Patten does. Be as absurd as you like.

One night I wrote to Mrs Thatcher.

King Kong.

All the chocolate manufacturers in Nottingham ... and so on.

Conversation with a Favourite Enemy

Some useful tips about how to be rude to people without actually starting a fight. It is also a poem about the magic, conquering power of poetry. I like the idea of the nightingale as a sort of poem-bomb, annihilating poets' enemies. Imagine some other useful weapons: the nuclear daffodil; the vertical take-off butterfly. Or list some nasty fates for your own worst enemies, preferably funny; and a few more, that aren't so funny. Poetry can be a vehicle for hatred, too. It may be better to work your bad feelings out in verse, and not on people.

Waves

A sort of footnote poem. Don't forget the diver. Think of some other cases that often miss their due measure of sympathy: the policeman making an arrest; the headmaster with a cane in his hand? ('This is going to hurt me more than it hurts you.') Well, I wonder. How about the lead singer, afraid the PA system isn't working? Or the surgeon performing the cancer operation?

Little Johnny's Confession

A poem written from the standpoint of a small child. It's a series of dramatic moments – they might almost be from a film – in the career of an infant criminal: the kill, the search, the waiting. Try a poem entitled *Little Johnny's Capture*, about what happens next. Do it from Little Johnny's own point of view again. Then try another from a policewoman's point of view. Try to make them comic and yet sad at the same time, as Patten does.

Philip Johnny's Confession

A poem written from the standpoint of a small child. It's a series of dramatic moments – they might almost be front a film – in the career of an infant criminal, the kid, the scarcely, the wanting. Try a poem entitled *Crime*. Write ... Crime, about what happens here. Do it from Philip Johnny's own point of view again. Then try another from a police woman's point of view. Try to make them come alive and yet read at the same time as *Butter, boss*.

Ai

Ai was born in 1947, two years after the atomic bomb was exploded on Hiroshima. One of her parents was black, and one Japanese. Her birth name was Florence Anthony, but she later adopted the writing name of Ai – pronounced ă (short), ēē (long) – as a sort of warcry. It should sound like the prelude to a Zulu charge. Ai's father was in the American army, and she spent much of her early life travelling. She was educated at the University of Arizona, where she received her BA in Oriental Studies. Later she did some teaching and worked as a fashion model. The flamboyant, and sometimes almost studied, violence of Ai's poetry seems a natural growth from this background and these interests. She says what she has to say with a gutsy directness of language, and at the same time with what can seem an almost Eastern inscrutability of tone. Galway Kinnell, himself one of the best poets in America, has called her 'the most talented young person I know'.

Starvation

Rain, tobacco juice, spit from the sky
shatters against your body,
as you push the pane of glass through the mud.
The white oak frame of the house shakes
when I slam the door and stand on the porch,
fanning myself with a piece of cardboard,
cut in the shape of a ham.

There's a pot of air on the stove.
You drove seventy miles, paid for that glass
and I can't remember the last good meal I had,
but bring it up here. I'll help you. I'm not angry.
We'll paint the sun on it from the inside,
so if we die some night, a light will still be on.
It's hell to starve in the dark.
I don't know why. I'm just your woman,
like you, crazy to lose all I've got.
It's rotten, you know, rotten.
The table's set. What time is it?
Wash your hands first. You're late.

I Have Got to Stop Loving You

So I have killed my black goat.
His kidney floats in a bowl,
a beige, flat fish, around whom parasites, slices of
      lemon,
break through the surface of hot broth, then sink below,
as I bend, face down in the steam, breathing in.
I hear this will cure anything.

When I am finished, I walk up to him.
He hangs from a short wooden post,
tongue stuck out of his mouth,
tasting the hay-flavored air.
A bib of flies gather at his throat
and further down, where he is open
and bare of all his organs,
I put my hand in, stroke him once,
then taking it out, look at the sky.
The stormclouds there break open
and raindrops, yellow as black cats' eyes, come down
each a tiny river, hateful and alone.

Wishing I could get out of this alive, I hug myself.
It is hard to remember if he suffered much.

The Cripple

I pull my legs from the floor,
as I would two weeds, gently,
pretending my roots have remained
in the soil that once held me upright
in the palm of its hand,
in the roads of black thread,
I walked, sowing years.
Instead, the itch deep in my heel
cries from its mouth one thorn after another.

Woman to Man

Lightning hits the roof,
shoves the knife, darkness,
deep in the walls.
They bleed light all over us
and your face, the fan, folds up,
so I won't see how afraid
to be with me you are.
We don't mix, even in bed,
where we keep ending up.
There's no need to hide it:
you're snow, I'm coal,
I've got the scars to prove it.
But open your mouth,
I'll give you a taste of black
you won't forget.
For a while, I'll let it make you strong,
make your heart lion,
then I'll take it back.

Child Beater

Outside, the rain, pinafore of gray water, dresses the
    town
and I stroke the leather belt,
as she sits in the rocking chair,
holding a crushed paper cup to her lips.
I yell at her, but she keeps rocking;
back, her eyes open, forward, they close.
Her body, somehow fat, though I feed her only once a
    day,
reminds me of my own just after she was born.
It's been seven years, but I still can't forget how I felt.
How heavy it feels to look at her.

I lay the belt on a chair
and get her dinner bowl.
I hit the spoon against it, set it down
and watch her crawl to it,
pausing after each forward thrust of her legs
and when she takes her first bite,
I grab the belt and beat her across the back
until her tears, beads of salt-filled glass, falling,
shatter on the floor.

I move off. I let her eat,
while I get my dog's chain leash from the closet.
I whirl it around my head.
O daughter, so far, you've only had a taste of icing,
are you ready now for some cake?

The Kid

My sister rubs the doll's face in mud,
then climbs through the truck window.
She ignores me as I walk around it,
hitting the flat tires with an iron rod.
The old man yells for me to help hitch the team,
but I keep walking around the truck, hitting harder,
until my mother calls.
I pick up a rock and throw it at the kitchen window,
but it falls short.
The old man's voice bounces off the air like a ball
I can't lift my leg over.

I stand beside him, waiting, but he doesn't look up
and I squeeze the rod, raise it, his skull splits open.
Mother runs toward us. I stand still,
get her across the spine as she bends over him.
I drop the rod and take the rifle from the house.
Roses are red, violets are blue,
one bullet for the black horse, two for the brown.
They're down quick. I spit, my tongue's bloody;
I've bitten it. I laugh, remember the one out back.
I catch her climbing from the truck, shoot.
The doll lands on the ground with her.
I pick it up, rock it in my arms.
Yeah, I'm Jack, Hogarth's son.
I'm nimble, I'm quick.

In the house, I put on the old man's best suit
and his patent leather shoes.
I pack my mother's satin nightgown
and my sister's doll in the suitcase.

Then I go outside and cross the fields to the highway.
I'm fourteen. I'm a wind from nowhere.
I can break your heart.

The Expectant Father

The skin of my mouth, chewed raw, tastes good.
I get up, cursing, and find the bottle of Scotch.
My mouth burns as darkess, lifting her skirt,
reveals daylight, a sleek left ankle.
The woman calls. I don't answer.
I imagine myself coming up to my own door,
holding a small reed basket in my arms.
Inside it, there is a child,
with clay tablets instead of hands,
and my name is written on each one.
The woman calls me again and I go to her.
She reaches for me, but I move away.
I frown, pulling back the covers to look at her.
So much going on outside;
the walls could cave in on us any time, any time.
I bring my face down
where the child's head should be and press hard.
I feel pain, she's pulling my hair.
I rise up, finally, and back away from the bed,
while she turns on her side
and drags her legs up to her chest.
I wait for her to cry,
then go into the kitchen.
I fix a Scotch and sit down at the table.
In six months, it is coming, in six months,
and I have no weapon against it.

Notes

Starvation

Most of Ai's poems are spoken by imaginary characters, but these characters tend to share a clipped, vicious utterance which makes them blood-sisters in a world raw with cruelty. Ai's first book was called *Cruelty*, and her themes – as here – tend to involve extremes of desire and hatred between human beings. Notice the wooden house in this poem, the long distance driving and the stove. It's an American – but a poor American – setting. Is the man coming home – home or to see her? – the woman's husband? Is that important? See what more you can guess or invent about the two people beyond what Ai tells you.

I Have Got to Stop Loving You

Is the black goat she kills just a goat? Or is there a suggestion that this dead beast is the man she has had to stop loving, and so has, in some way, wiped out of her mind, 'killed'? Is this idea too extreme? Or do you find it quite convincing? What about the sniffing of the goat's kidney? Does that sound like a herbal remedy to you, or is it the sort of thing a witch doctor would prescribe? Is this poem sick? Or is it deadly serious? Think how often we use phrases like: 'I'll kill you if you don't . . . *x, y or z*'. Try your own poem about ending a love affair. But make it a matter of tearing up, wiping out, as Ai does.

> I've drowned the pet cat you gave me,
>   it reminds me so much of you.

That sort of thing.

The Cripple

This one needs reading two or three times to get the meaning clear. The feeling ought to be clear after one reading. An itch with a mouth crying thorns might be difficult. What about the palm of the soil's hand, and the roads of thread? Are these comparisons – metaphors – too forced? What about the cliché 'beggars description' – originally from Shakespeare – isn't that forced, too? Try your own extreme metaphors. Make them absurd at first, then try to be more accurate: the windows of the classroom; the windows of the soul; the windows of perception; the windows of the telephone; the windows of the wind; the windows of the willows; the windows of the dog's paws. Which of these make sense? Do they all? If not, why not? If so, how? For instance couldn't the windows of the dog's paws draw attention to how sensitive the pads under the dog's feet are, so that it can feel things about the ground just as clearly as we can see things through panes of glass? Now think again about the others and then make up more metaphors of your own.

Woman to Man

Snow, coal; white man, black woman. Think about the idea of white lightning slicing through night's darkness. Is the poem too brutal, too despairing, or too proud? Is the woman too dominating? Try your own poem about a black man in bed with a white woman. Don't make it coarse. Focus on the ideas, the feelings. Where you want to say something physical, use a metaphor. For example: Ink on paper, milk with coffee.

Child Beater

Some background to the battered baby syndrome. Do you think there is something sadistic about this poem? Is the author almost in love with her own violence? Or is it all controlled and

167

directed to make a psychological point about the motive for beating children? Here the mother seems to be a kind of anorexic – she's afraid of being fat, and the chubby baby brings on these fears. The child is to be punished for eating – which she does rarely, anyway – by (to use an American phrase) having the shit beaten out of her. Try to write a reply to this poem from a child's point of view. Use very simple, seven-year-old's language. Keep it vivid and see if you can find a detail or two as good as 'pinafore of gray water'.

The Kid

Do you ever feel like the adolescent in the poem? Do you know people who do? Notice how fast the poem moves, like the action of a film. Indeed, there are films – *Badlands*, for example – which develop this kind of situation. Try writing a sequel, in the same narrative style. What happens to Jack next? Does he meet a girl like himself? Does he get arrested, or killed? See if you can create some contrasts with Paul Muldoon's *Immram* – in tone, in mood.

The Expectant Father

This is another male speaker poem. The idea of the coming child as an inevitable calamity has a kind of science fiction power. Notice once again how flatly Ai seems to write, and yet what depth she can squeeze out of her simple sentences. It was perhaps the novelist Ernest Hemingway, in books like *A Farewell To Arms*, who pioneered this directness, and it is now a central tradition in American writing. How do you think Kit Wright would have treated this theme? Could something be brought in by the humorous approach that the serious one leaves out? Have a try for yourself, perhaps with some comic rhyming. Then come back and admire the honesty and the driving force of Ai's treatment.

Paul Muldoon

The Irish poet Paul Muldóon, born in 1951, is the youngest
writer in this book. He has worked for some years as a Talks
Producer for the BBC, and his knowledge of radio, and the way
to make words sound right when spoken aloud, has undoubtedly
influenced the direct, clipped style of *Immram*. So, I think, at a
subterranean level, has the background experience of violence
through living in the war-stricken city of Belfast. Where a poet
lives, and what he or she does for a living, are always two
powerful influences on his or her choice of theme and method of
approach. When the place and the work meet, there can be a
fruitful soil for the growth of something really original, and
Immram marks a revival of the old-fashioned story-poem at a
time when no one else has seemed very interested in its
possibilities. But narrative is what grips the ordinary reader
most of all in a work of literature, and a good story can be told
with more vividness in verse than it can in prose. Try for
yourself. What about the story of Noah, or Jonah, from the
Bible? How would they sound in modern dress, and in verse?
Read Paul Muldoon's story-poem and see what ideas you can
pick up from him first.

Immram

I was fairly and squarely behind the eight
That morning in Foster's pool-hall
When it came to me out of the blue
In the shape of a sixteen-ounce billiard cue
That lent what he said some little weight.
'Your old man was an ass-hole.
That makes an ass-hole out of you.'
My grand-father hailed from New York State.
My grand-mother was part Cree.
This must be some new strain in my pedigree.

The billiard-player had been big, and black,
Dressed to kill, or inflict a wound,
And had hung around the pin-table
As long as it took to smoke a panatella.
I was clinging to an ice-pack
On which the Titanic might have foundered
When I was suddenly bedazzled
By a little silver knick-knack
That must have fallen from his hat-band.
I am telling this exactly as it happened.

I suppose that I should have called the cops
Or called it a day and gone home
And done myself, and you, a favour.
But I wanted to know more about my father.
So I drove west to Paradise
Where I was greeted by the distant hum
Of *Shall We Gather at the River?*
The perfect introduction to the kind of place
Where people go to end their lives.
It might have been *Bringing In the Sheaves*.

My mother had just been fed by force,
A pint of lukewarm water through a rubber hose.
I hadn't seen her in six months or a year,
Not since my father had disappeared.
Now she'd taken an overdose
Of alcohol and barbiturates,
And this, I learned, was her third.
I was told then by a male nurse
That if I came back at the end of the week
She might be able to bring herself to speak.

Which brought me round to the Atlantic Club.
The Atlantic Club was an old grain-silo
That gave onto the wharf.
Not the kind of place you took your wife
Unless she had it in mind to strip
Or you had a mind to put her up for sale.
I knew how my father had come here by himself
And maybe thrown a little crap
And watched his check double, and treble,
With highball hard on the heels of highball.

She was wearing what looked like a dead fox
Over a low-cut sequinned gown,
And went by the name of Susan, or Suzanne.
A girl who would never pass out of fashion
So long as there's an 'if' in California.
I stood her one or two pink gins
And the talk might have come round to passion
Had it not been for a pair of thugs
Who suggested that we both take a wander,
She upstairs, I into the wild, blue yonder.

They came bearing down on me out of nowhere.
A Buick and a Chevrolet.
They were heading towards a grand slam.
Salami on rye. I was the salami.
So much for my faith in human nature.
The age of chivalry how are you?
But I side-stepped them, neatly as Salome,
So they came up against one another
In a moment of intense heat and light,
Like a couple of turtles on their wedding-night.

Both were dead. Of that I was almost certain.
When I looked into their eyes
I sensed the import of their recent visions,
How you must get all of wisdom
As you pass through a wind-shield.
One's frizzled hair was dyed
A peroxide blond, his sinewy arms emblazoned
With tattoos, his vest marked *Urgent*.
All this was taking on a shape
That might be clearer after a night's sleep.

When the only thing I had ever held in common
With anyone else in the world
Was the ramshackle house on Central Boulevard
That I shared with my child-bride
Until she dropped out to join a commune,
You can imagine how little I was troubled
To kiss Goodbye to its weathered clapboard.
When I nudged the rocker on the porch
It rocked as though it might never rest.
It seemed that I would forever be driving west.

I was in luck. She'd woken from her slumbers
And was sitting out among flowering shrubs.
All might have been peace and harmony
In that land of milk and honey
But for the fact that our days are numbered,
But for the Foster's, the Atlantic Club,
And now, that my father owed Redpath money.
Redpath. She told me how his empire
Ran a little more than half-way to Hell
But began on the top floor of the Park Hotel.

Steel and glass were held in creative tension
That afternoon in the Park.
I strode through the cavernous lobby
And found myself behind a nervous couple
Who registered as Mr and Mrs Alfred Tennyson.
The unsmiling, balding desk-clerk
Looked like a man who would sell an alibi
To King Kong on the Empire State building,
So I thought better of passing the time of day.
I took the elevator all the way.

You remember how, in a half-remembered dream,
You found yourself in a long corridor,
How behind the first door there was nothing,
Nothing behind the second,
Then how you swayed from room to empty room
Until, beyond that last half-open door
You heard a telephone . . . and you were wakened
By a woman's voice asking you to come
To the Atlantic Club, between six and seven,
And when you came, to come alone.

I was met, not by the face behind the voice,
But by yet another aide-de-camp
Who would have passed for a Barbary pirate
With a line in small-talk like a parrot
And who ferried me past an outer office
To a not ungracious inner sanctum.
I did a breast-stroke through the carpet,
Went under once, only to surface
Alongside the raft of a banquet-table –
A whole roast pig, its mouth fixed on an apple.

Beyond the wall-length, two-way mirror
There was still more to feast your eyes upon
As Susan, or Susannah, danced
Before what looked like an invited audience,
A select band of admirers
To whom she would lay herself open.
I was staring into the middle distance
Where two men and a dog were mowing her meadow
When I was hit by a hypodermic syringe.
And I entered a world equally rich and strange.

There was one who can only have been asleep
Among row upon row of sheeted cadavers
In what might have been the Morgue
Of all the cities of America,
Who beckoned me towards her slab
And silently drew back the covers
On the vermilion omega
Where she had been repeatedly stabbed,
Whom I would carry over the threshold of pain
That she might come and come and come again.

I came to, under a steaming pile of trash
In the narrow alley-way
Behind that old Deep Water Baptist mission
Near the corner of Sixteenth and Ocean –
A blue-eyed boy, the Word made flesh
Amid no hosannahs nor hallelujahs
But the strains of Blind Lemon Jefferson
That leaked from the church
Through a hole in a tiny, stained-glass window,
In what was now a torrent, now had dwindled.

And honking to Blind Lemon's blues guitar
Was a solitary, black cat
Who would have turned the heads of Harlem.
He was no louder than a fire-alarm,
A full-length coat of alligator,
An ermine stole, his wide-brimmed hat
Festooned with family heirlooms.
I watch him trickle a fine, white powder
Into his palm, so not a grain would spill,
Then snort it through a rolled-up dollar bill.

This was angel dust, dust from an angel's wing
Where it glanced off the land of cocaine,
Be that Bolivia, Peru.
Or snow from the slopes of the Andes, so pure
It would never melt in spring.
But you know how over every Caliban
There's Ariel, and behind him, Prospero;
Everyone taking a cut, dividing and conquering
With lactose and dextrose,
Everyone getting right up everyone else's nose.

I would tip-toe round by the side of the church
For a better view. Some fresh cement.
I trod as lightly there
As a mere mortal at Grauman's Chinese Theatre.
An oxy-acetylene torch.
There were two false-bottomed
Station-waggons. I watched Mr See-You-Later
Unload a dozen polythene packs
From one to the other. *The Urgent Shipping Company*.
It behoved me to talk to the local P.D.

'My father, God rest him, he held this theory
That the Irish, the American Irish,
Were really the thirteenth tribe,
The Israelites of Europe.
All along, my father believed in fairies
But he might as well have been Jewish.'
His laugh was a slight hiccup.
I guessed that Lieutenant Brendan O'Leary's
Grand-mother's pee was green,
And that was why she had to leave old Skibbereen.

Now, what was all this about the Atlantic cabaret,
Urgent, the top floor of the Park?
When had I taken it into my head
That somebody somewhere wanted to see me dead?
Who? No, Redpath was strictly on the level.
So why, rather than drag in the Narcs.,
Why didn't he and I drive over to Ocean Boulevard
At Eighteenth Street, or wherever?
Would I mind stepping outside while he made a call
To such-and-such a luminary at City Hall?

We counted thirty-odd of those brown-eyed girls
Who ought to be in pictures,
Bronzed, bleached, bare-breasted,
Bare-assed to a man,
All sitting, cross-legged, in a circle
At the feet of this life-guard out of Big Sur
Who made an exhibition
Of his dorsals and his pectorals
While one by one his disciples took up the chant
The Lord is my surf-board. I shall not want.

He went on to explain to O'Leary and myself
How only that morning he had acquired the lease
On the old Baptist mission,
Though his was a wholly new religion.
He called it *The Way of The One Wave.*
This one wave was sky-high, like a wall of glass,
And had come to him in a vision.
You could ride it forever, effortlessly.
The Lieutenant was squatting before his new guru.
I would inform the Missing Persons Bureau.

His name? I already told you his name.
Forty-nine. Fifty come July.
Five ten or eleven. One hundred and eighty pounds.
He could be almost anyone.
And only now was it brought home to me
How rarely I looked in his eyes.
Which were hazel. His hair was mahogany brown.
There was a scar on his left forearm
From that time he got himself caught in the works
Of a saw-mill near Ithaca, New York.

I was just about getting things into perspective
When a mile-long white Cadillac
Came sweeping out of the distant past
Like a wayward Bay mist,
A transport of joy. There was that chauffeur
From the 1931 Sears Roebuck catalogue,
Susannah, as you guessed,
And this refugee from F. Scott Fitzgerald
Who looked as if he might indeed own the world.
His name was James Earl Caulfield III.

This was how it was. My father had been a mule.
He had flown down to Rio
Time and time again. But he courted disaster.
He tried to smuggle a wooden statue
Through the airport at Lima.
The Christ of the Andes. The statue was hollow.
He stumbled. It went and shattered.
And he had to stand idly by
As a cool fifty or sixty thousand dollars worth
Was trampled back into the good earth.

He would flee, to La Paz, then to Buenos Aires,
From alias to alias.
I imagined him sitting outside a hacienda
Somewhere in the Argentine.
He would peer for hours
Into the vastness of the pampas.
Or he might be pointing out the constellations
Of the Southern hemisphere
To the open-mouthed child at his elbow.
He sleeps with a loaded pistol under his pillow.

The mile-long white Cadillac had now wrapped
Itself round the Park Hotel.
We were spirited to the nineteenth floor
Where Caulfield located a secret door.
We climbed two perilous flights of steps
To the exclusive penthouse suite.
A moment later I was ushered
Into a chamber sealed with black drapes.
As I grew accustomed to the gloom
I realized there was someone else in the room.

He was huddled on an old orthopaedic mattress,
The makings of a skeleton,
Naked but for a pair of draw-string shorts.
His hair was waistlength, as was his beard.
He was covered in bedsores.
He raised one talon.
'I forgive you,' he croaked. 'And I forget.
On your way out, you tell that bastard
To bring me a dish of ice-cream.
I want Baskin-Robbins banana-nut ice-cream.'

I shimmied about the cavernous lobby.
Mr and Mrs Alfred Tennyson
Were ahead of me through the revolving door.
She tipped the bell-hop five dollars.
There was a steady stream of people
That flowed in one direction,
Faster and deeper,
That I would go along with, happily,
As I made my way back, like any other pilgrim,
To Main Street, to Foster's pool-room.

Notes

Immram

The first thing to say about this poem is: don't be put off by the
title. Imagine that it's called *A Mile-Long White Cadillac* or *Dust
From an Angel's Wing*. Now read on. Well, it wasn't too difficult,
was it? Take it fast and rap it out of the side of your mouth like
Humphrey Bogart playing a New York private eye. If you find it
difficult, go back and re-read it aloud, forgetting about the line
endings, the rhymes, the stanzas and, if you like, the hard bits of
the meaning. Just concentrate on getting the right tone of voice.
Pretend you're Kojak. Pretend you've just been given the star
role in a big American film. Pretend they mustn't know you're
really English. Did that help? I hope so.

Now that you've read the poem, some more detail may help
you get further into it. First of all, why is it called *Immram*? Well,
it's based on an eleventh-century Irish text, Immram Mael
Duin. (This, by the way, was translated by the Victorian poet,
Alfred Tennyson, in 1881. Hence the little joke about the couple
in the lift, appearing almost like the director Alfred Hitchcock
used to do in his own films.) An immram was a voyage-tale and
a story of revenge. In the Immram Mael Duin (or Voyage-Tale
of Mael Duin, or Muldoon) the hero sets out to avenge the
murder of his father by pirates. After a long voyage through the
fabulous islands of the western seas he eventually meets an old
hermit sitting on a rock, who advises him that revenge is really
pointless, whereupon Muldoon forgives and forgets his enemies
and sails for home. There's an element of Hamlet with a happy
ending about this tale, and it clearly attracted the poet in part
because it features one of his own ancestors. (An editor with the
name of MacBeth might easily want to rewrite the story of
Shakespeare's *Macbeth*, too. If so, where would he begin? By
using the modern figure of the Yorkshire Ripper perhaps?)

In bringing his own story up to date, Paul Muldoon has drawn on the style of the American gangster film, and in particular on the style of the American thriller writer, Raymond Chandler, who gave a special kind of elegance to the slangy talk of low-life San Francisco. As you'll see, if you turn back to the poem, it mixes in some very rich, and very grotesque, bits of phrasing alongside its contemporary wise-cracking. When the two cars crash, in the seventh section, we can all smile at the clever

They were heading towards a grand slam.
Salami on rye. I was the salami.

But the further idea that the colliding cars were

Like a couple of turtles on their wedding-night

adds a bit extra. It gives the picture a surrealist flavour, like something out of Salvador Dali. Many of the other details in the poem will only come clear with repeated readings. But here are one or two things to note. The old gang boss, Redpath, who is the modern poem's equivalent of the traditional hermit, is based on the American millionaire playboy, aviator and recluse Howard Hughes, who died in great isolation and squalor surrounded by armed guards to protect him from any intrusion on his privacy. The father in the poem had been involved in cocaine smuggling as a 'mule' or carrier, bringing 'snow' or cocaine, up from South America to the United States. Scott Fitzgerald was an American novelist of the 1920s who wrote about the rich. Much of the rest will be familiar to you from the cinema and television. Indeed, it's a poem – one of the few I know – which tries to use our common experience of a legendary landscape and legendary characters we know through film to replace the traditional legendary landscapes and characters earlier readers knew from the Bible, or from classical mythology. Does it come off, do you think? Or does it end up being too showy, too clever-clever?

Why not have a shot at something similar yourselves? It needn't be so long, of course. Try to make it a mixture: down-to-earth, jokey, and full of action, with a few complicated pieces to give more tone. Why not try something in the style of a James Bond film? What about the story of Jonah told as if Jonah was James Bond? Or a female Noah, from a Mills and Boon novel? Make the Flood sound romantic, and the whale like Blofeld. Use occasional rhymes – or near rhymes, they needn't be too exact – and count your lines into groups or sections of equal numbers. Then come back and read Paul Muldoon's poem again. You'll find you know it better, and you'll probably enjoy it more.

Afterword

I have arranged the poets in chronological order, starting with Lindsay and Lawrence and working forward to Ai and Muldoon. Indeed, a shorthand version of the book – in its main thematic drive – might reduce itself to these four poets. A good deal of what I would like users of the book to notice, think about, and imitate in their own writing, lies in the contrast between the raw and the smooth, the work of art and the slice of life. The slice of life can be shown to start with Lawrence, a European poet, and to end with Ai, an American one: the work of art can be studied in Lindsay, an American poet, and seen developed in Muldoon, a European one. In the intervening generations, Betjeman and Stevie Smith, Larkin and Hughes, Wright and Patten continue this fruitful contrast.

Work on any of these pairs would help to point up the two alternative larders of opportunity for the young poet about to bake his – or her – own poetic cake: the rough and natural ingredients of Lawrence, Smith, Hughes, Patten and Ai, the corked and refined materials of Lindsay, Betjeman, Larkin, Muldoon and Wright. Of course, these are extreme contrasts, and the book will have done no good if it fails to indicate more subtle connections: tightness in free verse, freedom in metre. In particular, the book will have missed its mark if it fails to start people writing for themselves. Almost every one of my notes aims to suggest a way of converting the text into a springboard for composition, so that English poetry can be gradually seen not as a heap of ruins, pompous and useless, but as the massive back-up force for each individual's own inspiration. I don't believe that writing poetry is more important than reading it. I believe that the two are part of the same process: the imaginative penetration of the world about us. Those who play the verse piano a little for themselves will always admire the great virtuosi.

Acknowledgements

We are grateful to the following for permission to reproduce copyright material:

George Allen & Unwin Ltd for the poems 'A Blade of Grass' & 'Sometimes it Happens' from *Vanishing Trick*, 'Somewhere Between Heaven & Woolworth's' & 'Little Johnny's Confession' from *Little Johnny's Confession*, 'The Wrong Number', 'Conversation with a Favourite Enemy' & 'Waves' from *Grave Gossip* all by Brian Patten; Faber & Faber Ltd for the poems 'Immram' from *Why Brownlee Left* by Paul Muldoon, 'Money', 'Annus Mirabilis', 'Homage to a Government' & 'The Old Fools' from *High Windows* by Philip Larkin, 'The Bull Moses' from *Lupercal*, 'A March Calf' & 'The Stag' from *Season Songs*, 'A Motorbike' & 'Beware of Stars' from *Moortown* all by Ted Hughes; Houghton Mifflin Co for the poems 'Starvation', 'I have got to stop Loving You', 'The Cripple', 'Woman to Man', 'Child Beater', 'The Kid' & 'The Expectant Father' from *Cruelty* by Ai, Copyright (c) 1970, 1973 by Ai; Literary Executor, James McGibbon for the poems 'Alfred the Great', 'Correspondence between Mr Harrison in Newcastle & Mr Shotto Peach Harrison in Hull', 'O Happy Days of England', 'Croft', 'The River God', 'Drugs Made Pauline Vague', 'The Engine Drain', 'The Hostage', 'The Past', 'Emily Writes such a good Letter', 'The Grange' & 'The Galloping Cat' from *The Collected Poems of Stevie Smith* pub. Allen Lane; The Marvell Press for the poems 'Born Yesterday', 'I Remember, I Remember' & 'Reasons for Attendance' from *The Less Deceived* by Philip Larkin; John Murray (Publishers) Ltd for the poems 'Summoned by Bells' from *Summoned by Bells*, 'Trebetherick', 'A Shropshire Lad', 'In Westminster Abbey', 'On a Portrait of a Deaf Man', 'Invasion Exercises on a Poultry Farm', 'Seaside Golf', 'Sun and Fun', 'Hunter Trials', 'False Security' & 'Executive' from *Collected Poems* by John Betjeman; the author, Kit Wright for his poems 'Every Day in Every Way', 'Red Boots On', 'A Doll's House', 'The Dark Night of the Sole', 'Elizabeth', 'The Other Side of the Moon' & 'Cold Up Here'.

We are grateful to the following for permission to reproduce photographs: George Allen and Unwin, page 146 (photo Nick Murphy); BBC Hulton Picture Library/Bettmann Archive, page xx; Faber and Faber, pages 112 (photo Mark Gerson) and 172; Houghton Mifflin Company, page 160 (photo Timothy Fuller): Nottingham University Library Manuscript Department, page 20 (photo Edward Weston); Universal Pictorial Press, pages 50, 72, 96 and 124.